"In the past 25 years, business ethics has become a growth industry, and its chief academic sponsors have been philosophers. Out of his long career as an executive in the field of investment, Edward Zinbarg believes that business ethicists have neglected 'the sense of compelling urgency that religious thinking can offer.' His book offers convincing evidence of this claim. He surveys six ancient religious traditions and demonstrates how their wisdom remains a rich source of reflection on moral questions in business. His finely balanced chapter 8, on new and old ethical challenges of 'globalization,' should be required reading for any Westerner about to do business in Asia."

—Donald W. Shriver, Jr., President Emeritus, Union Theological Seminary, New York, and former Adjunct Professor of Ethics, Columbia University School of Business Administration

"Edward Zinbarg doesn't write with the burden of a business leader defending his actions, an economist defending the discipline, or a student of ethics attempting to stay within the confines of that profession: he writes as a thoughtful person who has the benefit of having shouldered all three roles at one time or another. In doing so, he transcends the limitations of each singular perspective, while building on their possibilities, and forging their integration. In a similar way, Zinbarg expects that the reader will not hide behind any of these guises but come forward into dialogue, with an openness and honesty the subject so clearly merits. Faith, Morals, and Money *meets each of us where we are, and encourages us to do something remarkable: to take our whole selves with us, including our religious beliefs, when we go into the marketplace, either as a seller, buyer, employer, or employee. It's a radical argument, but in a book steeped in the realities of business life, it ultimately becomes a convincing, and perhaps even a life-altering proposition."*

—Cynthia A. Montgomery, Timken Professor of Business Administration, Harvard Business School

"A remarkable book. Edward Zinbarg provides his peers in the business community with the opportunity to listen afresh to the teachings they may have first learned on their parents' knees or in Sunday school, teachings which they may still honor but have neglected to practice in their everyday work. He also teaches us a surprising lesson, that the ethical imperatives of the world's great religions may be different but they are complementary."

—Peter Ochs, Edgar Bronfman Professor of Modern Judaic Studies, University of Virginia

"In this compelling and readable study, Edward Zinbarg argues that although ethical standards have been marginalized in mainstream economic theory, ethical situations abound in the practice of business. Toward redressing the gap between theory and practice, Zinbarg takes as axiomatic the continuing centrality of religion as the great reservoir of collective knowledge shaping and inspiring current quests for enduring marketplace ethics—even among those who see themselves beyond any religious system. Zinbarg lucidly presents ethical paradigms from both Eastern and Western religious traditions, and convincingly applies their wisdom to such perennial business issues as pricing, advertising and the conditions of employment. In this genuinely pluralistic examination, he illustrates how these diverse traditions share a historic understanding of market ethics as a fully integrated dimension of ethical life. Zinbarg has made a contribution to the critical process of reintegrating economic activity into our broader perspective of what it means to lead the just life—on both the individual and communal levels. A skillful blend of theory and case study, Faith, Morals,and Money *is at once an important inquiry and a powerful practical guide."*

—Karen Pechilis Prentiss, Associate Professor of Asian Religions, Drew University

—Christopher S. Taylor, Associate Professor of Religion and Islamic Studies, Drew University

Faith, Morals, and Money

FAITH, MORALS, AND MONEY

What the World's Religions Tell Us about Money in the Marketplace

EDWARD D. ZINBARG

Continuum
New York London

2001
The Continuum International Publishing Group Inc
370 Lexington Avenue, New York, NY 10017

The Continuum International Publishing Group Ltd
The Tower Building, 11 York Road, London SE1 7NX

Printed in the United States of America

Library of Congress Cataloging-in-Publication Data

Zinbarg, Edward D.
Faith, morals, and money : what the world's religions tell us about money in the marketplace / Edward D. Zinbarg.
p. cm.
Includes bibliographical references and index.
ISBN 0-8264-1342-0
1. Religious ethics. 2. Business ethics—Religious aspects. I. Title.
BJ1188 .Z56 2001
291.5'64—dc21

2001032566

To my grandchildren—
Amanda, Lori, Cory, Jesse, and Hayley—
in the hope that they will do right while doing well.

Contents

Preface

When you die, be sure nobody can say: "There goes a gonif."

IN YIDDISH, a *gonif* is a thief or, more broadly, a scoundrel; and this pungent statement sums up the ethical teaching my father drilled into me from my childhood until he died, all too soon, at age fifty-five. As a New York garment center manufacturer, my father spent his working life in an environment filled with *gonifs* of all religious and secular persuasions, but he was determined that he would not be one of them. Where did that determination come from? How did a street-smart kid who had quit school and gone to work in the roughneck garment center at age sixteen make that moral decision? My father claimed not to know how it happened, but I think I know.

My father was the son of a Torah scribe and his wife, a woman of deep Jewish faith. He rebelled against their ritually observant lifestyle and hence may not have recognized their influence on his thinking. Yet I believe they instilled in him a sense of being commanded—by a force beyond oneself and by a three-thousand-year tradition. The command was to treat people as beings created in the image of God, to avoid bringing shame on the Jewish community, and to seek the kind of immortality that comes from leaving behind a good name.

These were the moral imperatives, I think, that guided my father, both in his personal life and in the competitive marketplace. They made him aware that there must be boundaries between legitimate economic self-interest and being a *gonif*, a scoundrel. Those boundaries are the subject of this book. Let me describe briefly how it came to be written.

In 1994, I was approaching my sixtieth birthday. I was executive vice president of Prudential Insurance Company, where I had worked for almost thirty-five years. "The Pru" had been an American household name, trusted by generations of customers; and I had been proud of my association with it. But the Prudential name had recently become tainted by revelations of misleading sales practices.

While I was not in Prudential's marketing sector and thus had no direct responsibility for those practices, I was well acquainted with many of the executives involved and I felt a personal sense of shame by what they had done (or failed to do). At the same time, however, I was aware of many fraudulent claims against Prudential by policyholders who asserted damages that they never in fact sustained. So I knew that unethical behavior was present on both sides of the table.

As I pondered the ethical lapses of others, moreover, I became increasingly aware of my own. I realized that I had often treated people who worked for me as if they were mere machines. I recalled the words of a colleague who one day, in utter exasperation, said to me, "Ed, critiquing my performance is acceptable; making me feel worthless is not."

As a trained economist, author of investment textbooks, teacher of finance, and businessman, I am a champion of a competitive marketplace that rewards efficiency and effectiveness. Such a marketplace should be minimally restricted by edicts of government bureaucrats, who I believe are frequently motivated as much by a desire for power as by a desire for justice. But what about the edicts of personal moral conscience, like those of my father?

Most people, especially in the United States, acknowledge that religion played an important role in their moral upbringing. They learned the moral stories of their scriptures and heard the moral teachings of their sages. Their moral compasses could scarcely avoid being shaped by these experiences. Yet time after time, most people tell interviewers that religion does not significantly affect their daily business decisions. I wondered why.

Two possibilities occurred to me. One is that people may simply not understand that religion demands transformation—not only of one's inner being but also of one's outer behavior. That explanation seemed unlikely to me, since there is plenty of evidence that religion affects the way people behave in their private lives. A second, more likely possibility is that people understand the need for transformation but tend to see the marketplace as a unique realm, one in which religious ethics is not relevant.

Consider the content of most discussions of business ethics, whether in books and seminars or on the job and around the water cooler. How often do they speak to humanity's divine image or to ideas about immortality? How often does someone in a business discussion quote the Bible, or the *Qur'an,* or any other religious text or religious personality? Hardly ever! Religious ideas are usually considered too personal for public discourse and almost always inappropriate in a business setting.

I thought again about my father and about the reasons he went against the grain of garment-center morality. It became increasingly clear to me that I needed to study, write about, and speak about these issues in a way that I could not as an active member of a corporate hierarchy. I needed to learn—in some detail, not just in generalities—what the world's great religious traditions have had to say about the proper conduct of buyers and sellers, employers and employees, savers and borrowers, as they encounter each other every day in the marketplace. So, on October 24, 1994, my sixtieth birthday, I retired from Prudential to study, write, and speak out.

I will show in this book that there are many different theological starting points among the world's religious traditions, yet they reach remarkably similar conclusions about behavior in the marketplace. They are idealistic but not utopian. They accept a seller's need to put the best foot forward but don't excuse deliberate deceit. They recognize the hard realities of the workplace but teach that human beings should not be treated as if they were mere commodities. They caution against disparaging competitors, selling harmful products, price-gouging essential goods, and damaging the natural environment. They denounce bribery, call on professional people to be worthy of their clients' special trust in them, and ask lenders to be willing to suspend their legal rights in order to assist borrowers in distress. What a difference it would make if the vast numbers of people who go to synagogues, churches, mosques, and shrines on weekends and holy days brought even a fraction of the wisdom of their faiths to the weekday marketplace.

Jeffrey Stout has described my kind of research as *moral bricolage.* A *bricoleur,* he says in his book *Ethics after Babel* (pp. 74–75), "does odd jobs, drawing on a collection of assorted odds and ends available for use and kept on hand on the chance they might some day be useful." Stout argues that in most moral thinking, we need to be *bricoleurs*, "taking stock of problems that need solving and available conceptual resources for solving them . . . taking apart, putting together, reordering, weighting, weeding out, and filling in."

So this book constitutes a type of *moral bricolage.* I have sifted through many scriptures, commentaries, and histories of religious communities, trying to put together the pieces that emerged into a cohesive mosaic. Yet, as any handyman can attest, there are always other pieces available and different ways of putting them together. Consequently, I recognize that others may find different meanings than I have in the same material; still others may use different material; and still others may find my whole approach to be misguided. If so, I would welcome their thoughts.

EDZ
June 2001

Acknowledgments

I OFFER MY DEEP APPRECIATION to Professor Peter Ochs, formerly of Drew University and now at the University of Virginia. Since the day I first appeared in his office at Drew to tell him of my retirement study plans, he has been both mentor and friend—teaching me, reading and critiquing my thoughtful and less-thoughtful writing, encouraging me at every step of my journey. Professor Charles Courtney, also at Drew, gave me valuable counsel on the overall contents of this book; and my Continuum editor, Frank Oveis, has been a source of wisdom on the "packaging" of what I have to say.

The material on Jewish ethics benefited particularly from my studies with Rabbis David Novak and Neil Gillman, and from the wisdom of Rabbi Ismar Schorsch, Chancellor of The Jewish Theological Seminary, and Rabbi David Teutsch, President of the Reconstructionist Rabbinical College. Father John Langan and the Reverends Roger Badham, Donald Shriver, and Max Stackhouse enriched my understanding of Christian perspectives. Professor Chris Taylor and Imam Mokhtar Maghraoui provided incisive reviews of the material on Islamic ethics; and my work on the Eastern traditions could not have been done without the help of Professors Francisca Cho, Karen Pechilis Prentiss, Jacqueline Stone, and Tu Wei-ming.

I am very grateful to have been able to study in the intellectually challenging environments of Drew University, The Jewish Theological Seminary, and the Jewish Education Association of MetroWest, N.J. To have the resources of these fine institutions so readily available is indeed a privilege. Perhaps an even greater privilege is to have had the loving encouragement of the woman I cherish—my wife, Barbara.

PART I

THE MORAL CHALLENGE OF MONEY

As the world enters the twenty-first century, there is broad agreement that open, competitive markets add greatly to human well-being. At the same time, few would deny that the benefits come with a large ethical burden. Deceptive selling practices are widespread; employers often show little concern for their workers' human dignity; and breaches of trust are common.

These ethical issues may not bother some people, but they surely bother most. Participants in the marketplace are not only material calculating machines. They are beings with moral sensibilities. They resent deliberately misleading advertising, layoffs with little or no severance pay, and countless other economic realities that seem manifestly unfair. Yet most people also resent being told by faceless government officials what they may or may not do. Most people do not want a marketplace heavily burdened by bureaucratic rules and regulations.

To some extent, ethical costs are the price of freedom in the marketplace. The economy is most efficient when competition is open and unrestricted. But economic *efficiency* is often out of sync with economic *justice.* So a challenge of the twenty-first century is to figure out ways for the world to reap the benefits of spreading global competition while enduring fewer of its ethical costs—and to do this without growing interference by public officials into private economic decisions.

In the next two chapters, I will describe the way various "experts" have thought about this challenge. These include economists, philosophers, and sociologists. But they also include an important group of thinkers who tend to be ignored in most discussions of "real world" issues—issues such as truth in advertising or how to conduct a corporate downsizing. These thinkers are the men and women of the world's churches, synagogues, mosques, and shrines. To ignore them is to ignore the accumulated wisdom of thousands of years.

1

Are Markets and Morals Compatible?

> ***Hell, I don't know if it's fair.***
> ***I don't make the rules.***

THAT WAS THE RESPONSE Robert Allen, former chief executive of AT&T, gave to a reporter in 1996. The company had just announced a cost-cutting reorganization that might involve the layoff of forty thousand employees. The reporter asked Mr. Allen about the fairness of this corporate action, and he gave his answer in no uncertain terms.

Mr. Allen's answer might have been more tactfully phrased, but I will try to show in this chapter that it reflected some rather basic principles of modern democratic capitalism. These principles, I will argue, have great value; but they also have an important downside.

The Role and Rule of Law

As Mr. Allen indicated, we live in an era when the "rules" of the marketplace are supposed to be set not by individual conscience or by the cultural and religious traditions of the community but by formal legislative bodies. For example, suppose that Congress is worried about air pollution from certain kinds of factories and believes that the public is similarly concerned. In that case, Congress might pass laws requiring pollution prevention and cleanup devices in such factories, expecting that the costs of the devices will be incorporated into product prices. If consumers are willing to pay the higher prices, fine; the air will be cleaner. If not, they will be saying that the pollution laws are unacceptable and should be modified or repealed.

Mr. Allen probably believed that this is precisely what a free democratic society demands. Let society, through its elected representatives, set rules of marketplace "fairness" rather than expecting corporate CEOs like himself to do so. Why? Because only in this way can we know whether or not there is a social consensus about the ethics of the marketplace. Beyond this, the argument runs, there are only personal views about fairness, with no basis for evaluating one person's views against another's. It is dangerous to assume that a "higher moral law" exists outside of a nation's legislated civil and criminal codes. We separate church and state because different people will have different ideas about such ultimate truths and we don't want to pit one against the other outside of democratic processes.

It is significant, I think, that most of the highly publicized efforts by corporations to improve their ethical standards are aimed mainly at assuring *legal* compliance. For example, an article in the *Wall Street Journal* described a new division of a major international accounting firm whose mission is to help companies "create the moral organization" by means of "ethics process management." But did the developers of this ethics process management ask company suppliers, employees, and community representatives what constitutes a moral organization? No! According to the article, they went to company legal departments and asked what the "key risks" are. Not surprisingly, they got a list of potential legal violations.

Undoubtedly, a society ruled by democratic law is immeasurably preferable to one ruled by the arbitrary decisions of people with power. Yet it seems a shame that high-priced business consultants have to develop special processes simply to assure compliance with the law. Wouldn't it be nice if they worked on ways to encourage ethical behavior that goes beyond the letter of the law? But maybe this is all we should expect, for that is the way the economics profession has taught businesspeople like Robert Allen to think about the marketplace.

How Economists Have Confronted Moral Questions

If students in an economics class were asked to define "the marketplace," a correct answer would be: "It is a mechanism of competition and exchange that helps society achieve an efficient allocation of scarce resources." But suppose that a second question asked about the *morality* of the marketplace. Suppose, for example, that the students were asked to discuss the moral issues involved in a transfer of jobs from high-cost to lower-cost areas—say, from New York to South Carolina, or from the United States to South America.

A technically correct answer could be: The "principle of comparative advantage" is a well-accepted economic theory. According to that principle, the material well-being of society is maximized when people do what they are best at, or "least bad" at. Therefore, in the case at hand, we would need to investigate the comparative efficiency of the workers gaining and losing jobs, as measured by their output in relation to their wages. If the job transfer results in a net increase of efficiency, it improves society's material well-being and thus has positive moral value.

While this answer might be technically correct in most economics classes, professors in disciplines other than economics (and an occasional economics professor as well) surely would consider it incomplete. They would want the students to reflect on the possibility that efficiency may not be the only moral criterion in life, even in economic life. There might also be a criterion of equity, of fairness, of justice. Such considerations would require attention to the impacts on the various people involved and how these impacts balance out. How quickly will the workers losing jobs be able to find new jobs? How much value will be added to the owners of the business? Will the consumers of the company's products be better off after the change than before? The job transfer might well have positive moral value, but the facts required to defend its morality would go beyond simple comparative efficiency.

The existence of these two ways of thinking about economic activity—one wanting to focus solely on efficiency, the other wanting to consider the balancing of efficiency and equity—was highlighted when the 1998 Nobel Prize in economics was awarded to Professor Amartya Sen. The prize committee cited Professor Sen for his efforts to "restore an ethical dimension to the discussion of economic problems." *Restore?* Had ethics gotten lost at some point from economists' discussions?

Regrettably, it had. Indeed, Sen told a reporter that when he himself was a young student of Professor Joan Robinson, one of the giants of modern economic theory, she had advised him to "forget all that ethics rubbish." As it turned out, he ignored her advice and went on to win the Nobel Prize for his ethical restorative work. However, many earlier winners of the Nobel economics award had made their mark in rather strict adherence to Professor Robinson's dictum. Their work reflected a common view of economists that moral discourse is not directly relevant to their profession.

Clearly this was the context of Robert Allen's response about the fairness of his company's actions. He had been trained to concern himself with economic efficiency. Fairness was the concern of others. He did not "make the rules." But how did economic efficiency and economic morality become separated?

Markets and Morals in the History of Economic Thought

Until the Industrial Revolution made its earliest stirrings in sixteenth-century Europe, society had been governed largely by top-down, church-dominated rules of behavior. These rules included an idea of "just prices." Human justice, economic justice, and economic efficiency were not distinct from each other in those days.

Charging more than something was "worth," simply because someone might be willing to pay the price, seemed immoral to church leaders. In their view, an item was worth the labor value embedded in producing it and bringing it to market. The value of that labor, in turn, was a function of the social rank of the laborer, which, at least to some degree, reflected the quality of his education and skills. Moreover, only those items that satisfied normal or "natural" wants were deemed to have value. Thus, for the church, prices had a strong moral dimension. Prices were a matter of "justice," not of simple supply and demand, and this mind-set was similar in non-European societies as well.

As the sixteenth century unfolded, the marketplace became more decentralized and more secular. Students of the changing economic scene began to understand that the prices of goods and services *must* reflect the desires of buyers and sellers. They began to understand, albeit vaguely, that all prices are, in fact, interdependent—because one man's price is another's cost, and because consumers can substitute one product for another. This was increasingly a fact of life whether the clergy liked it or not.

During the century that followed these early, rather informal observations of the way markets work, Sir Francis Bacon and other scientists were developing new ways of understanding the way nature works. They insisted that theory should not be based on casual observation. It should be based on, and tested against, careful measurements of the things one is trying to understand.

This approach to the study of nature encouraged students of economic society to use similar methods. So they developed statistics on population, on the quantity of land use, and on society's income and expenses. Based on these data, they formulated theories of value that reflected land as well as labor inputs (they did not yet have a good way to take capital and entrepreneurship into account) and theories about the relationships between production and consumption.

The Role of Self-Interest

As these ideas were developing, the philosopher Thomas Hobbes put forth a theory of human nature in his most famous work, *Leviathan*, published in 1651. Hobbes argued that self-interest is the most powerful of human motivations—so powerful a drive that people will do almost anything to satisfy it, including aggressive acts against their neighbors. Consequently, he said, the only way that society could survive peacefully would be for people to submit to an authoritarian government that would restrain their baser instincts.

For many students of the marketplace, Hobbes's argument represented a major challenge. For while they agreed that self-interest is a powerful motivator of economic behavior, they did not see it as a destructive force. To the contrary, they argued that self-interest causes people to engage in the kinds of work and the kinds of consumption that best match their skills and preferences. This causes economic output to grow and fosters the best mix of what is produced. Thus, they said, self-interest can enhance social well-being.

Based on their belief that economic self-interest can be beneficial rather than harmful to society, these students of the marketplace argued (against Hobbes) that the role of government should not be to shackle self-interest. Rather, government should help channel it toward national objectives. Not least of such objectives, in their view, was to increase the stock of gold and other precious metals in the state treasury. This type of governmental policy came to be referred to as "mercantilism."

Adam Smith Enters the Scene

In 1776, Adam Smith's landmark *Inquiry into the Nature and Causes of the Wealth of Nations* (generally referred to as *The Wealth of Nations*) was published. It was a time of growing recognition that government efforts to regulate economic activity often produced results quite the opposite of those intended. It was seen, for example, that when governments tried to help the common man by forcing down the prices of food and other essential goods, the result was more often shortages and black markets than benefits to consumers. As for the mercantilist goal of increasing the national stockpile of precious metals, people began to argue that a better goal would be to increase the material well-being of ordinary citizens.

It was Smith's genius to organize a discussion of these emerging themes in the context of examples of how they played out in familiar everyday commercial and political life. Most of us know about his doctrine of the "invisible hand." This concept says, in effect, that as each person pursues his or her own economic self-interest, with a minimum of government interference, the greatest material good for the greatest number in society will tend to be produced. Smith's *laissez faire*—leave them alone—attitude did not reflect a lack of concern about society's well-being. Rather, he was profoundly skeptical about the wisdom and motivation of public officials who try to regulate economic activity.

Moreover, Smith discussed these themes not only as a political and economic analyst but also in his role as a professor of moral philosophy at the University of Glasgow. In addition to *Wealth of Nations*, he wrote a major philosophical treatise called *Theory of Moral Sentiments*. In it he argued that most people understand that their self-interest and personal happiness require the approval of others. This approval, he asserted, is earned most effectively and most consistently when one behaves empathetically and controls one's baser passions.

Smith believed strongly that the quest for the approval of others, particularly of one's peers, shows up in the marketplace as well as in more personal relationships. He understood, moreover, that most sensible businesspeople realize that their firms will thrive or fail on the basis of repeated transactions, not just the transaction of the moment. Therefore, the quest for approval in the eyes of others must be an ongoing one, and the market thus becomes an effective mechanism for channeling self-interest in directions that benefit the whole society.

Economic Thought after Adam Smith

During most of the nineteenth century, economists subtly shifted from the humanistic, holistic approach of Adam Smith to one of abstract deductive reasoning from "simplifying assumptions." They believed that all truly important economic phenomena could be represented in quantitative terms and could be analyzed in the same way as natural phenomena in the physical sciences. As for the motivations and other human dimensions of the phenomena they were observing, those were issues for philosophers and theologians, not for economists.

Not every noteworthy economic observer of the period agreed with this line of reasoning. For example, Karl Marx tried to explain the widespread poverty of working people by focusing on efforts by employers to pay laborers less than the values produced; and he advocated radical social reform. But he and others with similar views were viewed by the prominent economists of the day as political propagandists rather than as "economic scientists." They had little impact on mainstream economic analysts, who continued to pay scant attention to the social and ethical dynamics of human economic behavior.

Economists' inattention to ethical issues was reinforced during the twentieth century by the application of advanced mathematics and electronic computers to their work. These tools permitted a wide variety of economic hypotheses to be tested. Yet those hypotheses continued to ignore most influences on human economic behavior that could not be quantified.

Economists do not deny the existence of "noneconomic" influences on marketplace behavior—such as power relationships, social ties within families and communities, and ethical sensibilities. In fact, a splinter group within the profession, calling themselves "behavioral economists," has tried to demonstrate statistically the existence of these influences. These behavioral economists are finally being taken fairly seriously by their more mainstream colleagues, as evidenced on April 27, 2001, when the American Economic Association gave its prestigious John Bates Clark award to Matthew Rabin, a young professor who, among other innovative uses of economic data, has shown mathematically that people often make economic decisions based on their perceptions of fairness and reciprocity, even when such decisions do not maximize their material well-being. Of course, most noneconomists never needed mathematical proof of this aspect of human behavior; but even now that the economics profession has the proof, most practitioners insist on referring to these behavioral influences as "externalities." They should be thought about separately rather than being considered an integral part of the economic system.

The author of one of the most widely adopted textbooks on Principles of Economics recently highlighted this theme. He told a newspaper reporter that modern economists make a distinction between statements that are scientifically verifiable and statements that reflect value judgments. He used the study of income inequality as an example, noting that the amount of inequality can be objectively measured and that some possible sources of the inequality—such as levels of education—can be objectively measured and tested. What cannot be objectively measured and tested, he said, is the sense of insecurity among people with different income levels and the impact of different levels of insecurity on social cohesion. He compared an economist's role to that of a doctor who has a duty to explain what will happen if a cancer patient is removed from chemotherapy treatment. According to this economist, the doctor should leave it to others—such as ministers, legislators, and philosophers—to struggle with the moral question of whether to actually stop the treatment.

As in the nineteenth century, the twentieth century produced dissenters from this amoral approach to economics, who voiced their qualms about excessive abstraction—even while engaging in it. For example, John Maynard Keynes's monumental *General Theory of Employment, Income and Money* tried to explain the Great Depression by employing a series of mathematical constructs—such as the "marginal propensity to consume." Yet Keynes is reported to have written, in a personal letter to the Archbishop of Canterbury, that ethics is at the heart of governmental economic policy. Accordingly, he told the archbishop, it is quite appropriate for the church to "interfere in what is essentially a branch of ethics."

Keynes's acknowledgment notwithstanding, ethics remains an "externality" in most modern economic theories. Amartya Sen has been called "the conscience of the economics profession." But isn't it sad that the economics profession should need a maverick with a conscience because it seems not to possess one of its own? I'm not suggesting that the profession is immoral. It is neither moral nor immoral, but *amoral*; and, as a card-carrying member of the profession, I am saddened by this aspect of its evolution.

Perhaps even more saddening is the frequency with which an *amoral* approach to economics reflects the attitude of entire universities. Recently, a chaplain at one of America's most prestigious universities recalled a convocation of 1,000 first-year students. At this assembly, the former chairman of the political science department told the students that they could expect their education to provide them with an understanding of how to search rigorously for facts, for data. But, the chaplain lamented, the students were told rather clearly not to expect ethical guidance from their course work. This university, the speaker insisted, is totally *amoral.*

Business Impact of an "Amoral" Economics Profession

Since this is the kind of economics taught in most schools, where does it leave people who want to apply principles of economic efficiency to their activities but also wonder about moral issues other than the efficient allocation of scarce resources? Where does it leave the business manager, the employee, the investor, the consumer shopping in the stores, when he or she is asked: Is what you are about to do "right"? It leaves them where Robert Allen was when he said, "Hell, I don't know if it's fair. I don't make the rules." It leaves them in the position of the public relations officers of companies accused of making misleading statements to customers. All too often they say, "Our company did nothing against the law" rather than "Our company did not make misleading statements."

Is it true that only a Congressional debate can reveal whether there is a consensus about right and wrong behavior in the marketplace? That question has been raised not only by political "liberals" but also by such "neo-conservatives" as Irving Kristol.

Two Cheers for Capitalism is the ironic title of a book by Kristol. He is a strong believer in democratic capitalism, which he describes as a market-based system of production and distribution by politically free human beings. He argues that this system contained three basic promises (p. 257). The first was "continued improvement in the material conditions of all its citizens, a promise without precedent in human history." The second was "an equally unprecedented measure of individual freedom for all of these same citizens." Finally, he says, democratic capitalism held out "the promise that, amidst this prosperity and liberty, the individual could satisfy his instinct for self-perfection—for leading a virtuous life that satisfied the demands of his spirit (or, as one used to say, his soul)—and that the free exercise of such individual virtue would aggregate into a just society."

But Kristol gives capitalism only two cheers, rather than three, because of its shortfall on the third of these promises. He takes issue with the treatment of moral concerns by many champions of democratic capitalism, including another Nobel Prize winner, Friedrich von Hayek. Kristol both approves of, and is disturbed by, a central argument that Hayek makes, namely, that in a free society the rewards to each individual must be in proportion to one's "success" rather than to one's "moral merit." This is not because Hayek disparages moral merit or quarrels with the notion that justice calls for some proportionality between rewards and moral merit. The problem, he says, is that there always will be vast differences of opinion about how to define and measure moral merit. In a free society, he insists, no single person or group of persons can be empowered to make such judgments. It is the same argument implicit in Robert Allen's response to the question of whether AT&T's actions were "fair."

Hayek's theme is echoed by a man who is one of the best-known exponents of free markets worldwide, another Nobel Prize winner, Milton Friedman. Among Friedman's many publications is one entitled *Free to Choose,* co-authored with his wife. The first chapter of this book is called "The Power of the Market," and it contains the following statement (p. 27):

> Narrow preoccupation with the economic market has led to a narrow interpretation of self-interest as myopic selfishness, as exclusive concern with immediate rewards. Economics has been berated for allegedly drawing far-reaching conclusions from a wholly unrealistic "economic man" who is little more than a calculating machine, responding only to monetary stimuli. That is a great mistake. Self-interest is not myopic selfishness. It is whatever it is that interests the participants, whatever they value, whatever goals they pursue. The scientist seeking to advance the frontiers of his discipline, the missionary seeking to convert infidels to the true faith, the philanthropist seeking to bring comfort to the needy—all are pursuing their interests, as they see them, as they judge them by their own value.

Since the index to Friedman's book contains not a single entry such as "ethics," "morality," "justice," or "fairness," one cannot be sure if this statement reflects his views about the relationship of morality to the economic marketplace. But if it does, it is a rather curious set of views. On the one hand, there is a suggestion that "whatever people value" is equally moral in his mind. On the other hand, the illustrations of scientist, missionary, and philanthropist suggest that he has rather traditional views of what kinds of activity are "good." However, he does not tell us whether any activities might be "bad," even if legal. His failure to address moral issues in a book called *Free to Choose* does not mean that Friedman is himself amoral, much less immoral, which I am certain he is not. Rather, it suggests that he fully agrees with the central thrust of modern economic thought—that is, such issues are for others to be concerned with.

Irving Kristol acknowledges that economists like Hayek, Friedman, and others of similar disposition make an admirable antitotalitarian argument, and may even be correct in their reading of what is feasible in a democratic society. But Kristol maintains that they are incorrectly counterpointing a *free* society against a *just* society by saying, in effect, that while we know what freedom is, we have no generally accepted knowledge of what justice is because we have no generally accepted understanding of ethical behavior or moral merit. That is a claim I will challenge in the next chapter—and, indeed, in the rest of this book—as I explore the attitudes of the world's major religious traditions toward marketplace ethics.

2

Why Bring Religion into the Picture?

> ***The Catholic Church should stick to religion and we'll stick to advertising.***

THAT'S WHAT THE HEAD of a New York ad agency said when the Catholic Pontifical Council for Social Communications published a set of guidelines on the use of sexual material in advertising. Apparently it did not occur to him—or it did, but he would not admit it in public—that all advertising has moral implications and that all religions are concerned with morality.

Advertisers try to make their products seem desirable to ad viewers. So they naturally put a positive spin on the verbal and pictorial information contained in their ads. But this effort necessarily raises moral issues, because the information can be misleading, disparaging of competitors, or disrespectful of various groups of people.

Since the content of all advertising has moral implications, why shouldn't people who are particularly interested in moral issues—as Catholic clergy and other religious leaders surely are—speak out about things such as the use of sexuality in ads? As I suggested in the preceding chapter, the answer likely to be given by most modern economists (and, apparently, by at least some heads of ad agencies) is that the church's opinion about sexual ethics is simply one of many, and no one can say which opinion is best. Therefore, unless a law is passed about the use of sexual material in advertising, advertisers should do as they please, without interference. Some might add that, in a secular society, the interference of a religious institution is particularly inappropriate.

These are ill-advised reactions. True, religion does not have a monopoly on ethical insight, and religious leaders have no right to force their views on anyone. But religions do have a very long history of thinking about ethical issues—a far longer history than advertising or other business executives have. It is noteworthy that Friedrich von Hayek, the Nobel Prize–winning economic libertarian I cited in the preceding chapter, a man who is doubtful that many common standards of moral merit exist in the world, acknowledges the crucial role that religions have played in the development of whatever standards do exist. In *The Fatal Conceit: The Errors of Socialism*, Hayek writes (p. 137): "Even those among us, like myself, who are not prepared to accept the anthropomorphic conception of a personal divinity ought to admit that the [absence of religious belief] would have deprived mankind of a powerful support in the development of the extended order that we now enjoy."

It seems to me that religious people not only have a right to speak out on the ethical implications of economic behavior; they have a responsibility to do so. Indeed, they have a special responsibility to say that religious standards of morality apply not only to utterly horrible behavior, like genocide, for example, but also to everyday behavior in the marketplace.

Do Common Ethical Standards Exist?

Michael Walzer is a philosopher, not an economist. But when he discusses ethics, as he does in his book *Spheres of Justice*, he sounds a good deal like most modern economists. "Justice is a human construction," he says (pp. 5-6), observing that such ethically charged words as health, danger, old age, unemployment, and poverty have different meanings in different cultures and in particular historical time periods. This way of looking at the world reflects a recent tendency in the world of philosophy that parallels an earlier development in the world of economics. It is called *postmodern* philosophy.

The European Enlightenment had led people in the Western world to search for universal principles of behavior that any rational person would accept. Adam Smith searched for such principles in both material and moral behavior. Most of his successors gave up on finding universal principles of economic morality but thought they found some in the purely material sphere. It was the "doctrine of the economic man." It asserted that when people come to the marketplace, either as buyers or sellers, they are almost totally focused on maximizing their material wealth and minimizing the material costs of achieving that goal.

It took philosophers a while to catch up with economists, but the ones who did, the so-called postmodern philosophers, did so with breathtaking vigor. One of them, Richard Rorty, goes so far as to say that any mode of behavior is acceptable as long as it involves persuasion rather than force. Even this qualification, moreover, does not reflect the existence of some natural law against the use of force. No, the need for persuasion rather than force is simply a pragmatic recognition that force puts an end to social relationships.

James Q. Wilson is neither an economist nor a philosopher but a sociologist. From that vantage point, he concludes that human behavior conforms neither to the Enlightenment's vision of a broad range of universal standards nor to the postmodern claim that there are no common standards at all. Instead, he takes a commonsense middle-ground position. In a book called *The Moral Sense*, he argues (pp. 225–26) that there are few, if any, universal ways *to apply* moral principles; that depends on particular economic circumstances and social structures. But a wide variety of applications, he says, by no means indicate an equally wide variety of underlying principles. These, he claims, are clearly present in human behavior.

It is striking, Wilson says, that when people behave in a way that violates what seem to be generally understood principles of appropriate behavior, they usually offer excuses other than "I did it just because I wanted to." An example of Wilson's point in the economic sphere can be found in the daily newspapers, when business executives are asked to respond to charges that they are exploiting sweatshop laborers. They never say, "That's what we want to do, so we do it." Instead, they claim that they don't really treat their employees as badly as their critics claim, or that they're forced to do it because they wouldn't be able to match their competitors' prices if they didn't.

The very fact that sweatshop employers feel a need to make excuses suggests that they understand as well as their critics what moral behavior means. Coming back to my opening example, is there any real doubt that the advertising executive who told the Catholic Church to butt out of his affairs doesn't know that blatant sexual exhibitionism violates long-accepted common standards of decency? There may not be universal moral standards covering all situations, but there surely are many that most people would acknowledge. The issue is not an absence of moral standards; it's a lack of adherence to the standards.

Religious Ethics and Economic Behavior

This book is about the gaps that exist between religious ethics and the way people behave in the marketplace. It concentrates on behavior in the marketplace because, when money is at stake, people do things that they would rarely do otherwise. And it concentrates on religious ethics because most people, whether they are conscious of it or not, derive many of their basic ethical understandings from their religious training. Countless studies have shown that this is true even of people who are not closely affiliated with an organized religious institution.

The earliest ethical lessons most people in the world are taught refer to God's commands, or to the examples of exalted religious figures like Jesus, or Muhammad, or the Buddha. These lessons become embedded in their psyches, even if they go on to study what philosophers such as Aristotle or Immanuel Kant had to say about ethics. While some have feared, and others have hoped, that modernity would lead to a withering away of religion as an important element of human existence, this has not happened. Religion remains one of the key defining characteristics of the world's communities.

Not only is the worldview of most people shaped importantly by their religious training; I will show in this book that the ethical lessons of the world's religions are quite similar despite widely differing theologies. Moreover, I believe, and surveys show, that most people do apply the ethical standards of their religious traditions in their relationships with family and friends. But when money is at stake, even ties of family and friendship get torn asunder, much less relationships with strangers.

Ironically, there has been an explosion of religious study groups at workplaces all across the United States. Yet a recent *Business Week* cover story on the subject deals almost entirely with the "spiritual quest" of the participants. There is little mention of any effort by the participants to ask each other what their religious traditions say about the business decisions they have to make every day.

A parallel phenomenon exists among businesspeople who claim to be deeply "spiritual" and, at the same time, are antagonistic to "religion." In their recent *Spiritual Audit of Corporate America*, Ian Mitroff and Elizabeth Denton surveyed a cross-section of business managers and found that 60 percent described religion with such words as "formal, dogmatic, intolerant, and dividing people more than bringing them together." In contrast, spirituality was seen as "informal, personal, universal, non-denominational, broadly inclusive, and tolerant." Understandably, the managers holding these views considered religion to be "a highly inappropriate topic and form of expression in the workplace." Yet "spirituality was viewed as highly appropriate."

Significantly, the respondents to this survey focused heavily on the inner dimensions of spirituality. "Very few made any mention at all" of the outer dimensions that consider how a person's actions affect other people. I wish the interviewers had asked whether these managers thought of such people as Martin Luther King, Jr., Mother Teresa, Abraham Joshua Heschel, Mahatma Gandhi, or the Dalai Lama as spiritual but not religious, concerned with the inner but not outer dimensions of life. I wonder whether the respondents would have denied that the religious faith and the spirituality of these people were inextricably intertwined, and that they could hardly have expressed their spirituality without revealing its religious sources and its implications for ethical behavior.

Most business managers acknowledge that religion played an important role in their moral upbringing. Yet few say that religion significantly affects their daily business decisions. And a recent statistical comparison between religious belief, on the one hand, and attitudes toward corporate social responsibility, on the other, revealed almost no correlation. Somehow the message hasn't gotten through to people that their religious faith—or their spirituality, if they prefer to call it that—demands attention to their outer economic lives as well as to their inner spiritual lives.

Like the advertising executive, many people may fear that introducing religious ethics into the marketplace risks upsetting the delicate balance between private faith and the public domain. Indeed, in a book called *The Culture of Disbelief*, Stephen Carter makes the following claim (p. 3): "In our sensible zeal to keep religion from dominating our politics, we have created a political and legal culture that presses [even] the religiously faithful to be other than themselves, to act publicly, and sometimes privately as well, as though their faith does not matter to them."

Discussions of religious ethics in our day are, at most, confined to "big picture issues," such as homelessness, gun control, or biomedical issues. Here the views of theologians are at least considered if not embraced. But how often have you heard clergymen or women preach about the applicability of their religion's ethics to shopping at the supermarket or managing employees? Not often, I suspect. Indeed, the Catholic pronouncement on advertising is a notable exception rather than a common occurrence. One reason may be that many clerics feel insufficiently informed about the business world to be confident about connecting religious ethics to such matters. But another may be that they don't want to risk offending their congregants.

Tragic experience does, of course, indicate that when religion enters the public sphere it can lead to oppression rather than to insight and virtue. Freedom requires that no religious group should be able to impose its own moral understandings on the populace at large. All people must participate in developing the moral understandings by which they will live. But freedom allows, and justice requires, that voices be heard which urge participants in the global marketplace not to divorce their daily behavior from their moral understandings.

Since moral understandings are derived from religious traditions as well as from secular education, the voices that speak to the issue should be religious as well as secular. Alan Wolfe, a sociologist who has done numerous surveys of American attitudes about politics, religion, and other aspects of daily life, observes in a new book entitled *Moral Freedom: The Search for Virtue in a World of Choice* that Americans "want faith and freedom simultaneously." They respect the teachings of their religious traditions, but they want to be active participants in interpreting, applying, and sometimes redefining the rules meant to guide them.

I totally agree. That's what this book is about. It is about interpreting, applying, and sometimes redefining the teachings of the world's great religious traditions—teachings not only about big-picture issues but also about the more nitty-gritty issues of the marketplace. It is issues such as conditions of employment and propriety in advertising that are key to the question of whether the marketplace can be a more ethical arena while it remains a vibrant competitive mechanism for the efficient allocation of scarce resources.

PART II

FAITH AND MONEY: THE UNDERPINNINGS OF RELIGIOUS ETHICS

THE MAJOR RELIGIOUS TRADITIONS of the West and East have rather different worldviews and, hence, different approaches to ethical issues. Those of the West—Judaism, Christianity, and Islam, to name them in the chronological order of their development—trace their origins to the vision of a man called Abraham, some four thousand years ago. It was a vision of a single God who created the universe and all within it. While the three religious communities that evolved from that vision are different in many respects, they can be grouped together because of the beliefs they hold in common.

In addition to their belief in a single Creator God, the three "Abrahamic" faiths assert that God revealed himself to humanity through chosen messengers and commanded people to live in a certain way. They also claim that God is active in history, a history that not only had a beginning, when God created the universe, but also will have an end. At that ending of history, they believe, God will establish a divine kingdom of justice and mercy. In the meantime, however, until God establishes his kingdom, all three religions assert that human beings have the freedom to do or not do what God wants of them. And what God wants is for men and women not only to revere him but to do all they can to correct the imperfections of their earthly abode.

Remarkably, far to the east of Abraham's world, and at almost the same time, the Aryan settlers of the Indian subcontinent and the Chinese emperors of the Shang dynasty were also responding in unique ways to their sense of the divine. Two major religious streams, Hinduism and Buddhism, flowed from the Indian origin, while Confucianism became a central tradition in China.

These Eastern traditions are not monotheistic; indeed some do not refer to "god" at all. They tend to be more naturalistic, stressing a mystical sense of harmony among the human and nonhuman aspects of the universe. A creation–revelation–redemption sequence, typical of the Abrahamic faiths, is not a central feature of Eastern religious worldviews.

In their moral outlook, Eastern traditions tend to see evil as a reflection *more* of ignorance than of the existential struggle between good and bad impulses portrayed by the Abrahamic faiths. When human ignorance is overcome, according to the Eastern view, moral individuals and moral societies can prevail.

Thus, the religious ethics of the West have their origin in God's commands, whereas Eastern religious ethics originate in human wisdom itself. As I will show in the next two chapters, their combined ethical understandings offer an inspiring vision of a life well led.

3

Divine Command Traditions of the West

The Jewish Heritage

Did you deal faithfully?

A famous passage in the Talmud says that when a man appears in heaven for final judgment, he is asked three questions. Did you deal faithfully? Did you set aside regular time for study? Did you have children? While the second and third questions refer to very obvious Jewish values—knowledge of scripture and continuity of the community—scholars have discussed what the first question refers to. Their conclusion is that it refers to business dealings.

Imagine! The very first question a heavenly inquisitor supposedly asks a person is whether that person was honest in business affairs. This shows how much importance Judaism gives to ethics in the marketplace. The rabbinic sages pointed to Leviticus 25:14, which says: "When you sell property to your neighbor, or buy any from your neighbor, you shall not wrong one another." From it they concluded that "if one is honest in his business dealings and people esteem him, it is accounted to him as though he had fulfilled the whole Torah."

There is much truth in the common view that Judaism is less a system of theological beliefs than a system of behaviors—ritual, familial, and communal behaviors. Yet I think the behaviors reflect a certain theological worldview. That worldview cannot be encapsulated in a creed, a set of dogmas. But, for me at least, its central theme is that the sacred and the secular are interlocked. It urges that secular behavior should be endowed with a sacred dimension.

I realize that many Christians think Jesus originated this integration of the sacred and the secular. My own sense is that he was carrying forward the tradition he had inherited. The many commandments of the Hebrew Bible are striking in their juxtaposition of an Israelite's obligations both to God and to his fellows—indeed, to all of God's creation, as when Deuteronomy (22:6) enjoins the removal of baby birds or eggs from the nest in the presence of the mother bird.

Abraham Joshua Heschel, one of the most loved and respected clergymen of modern times, was fond of saying that "Jews insist on the deed and pray for the intention." But he had a twinkle in his eye as he spoke the words. For neither he nor his rabbinic ancestors really made a distinction between right action, right belief, and right intention. The basic issue, Heschel wrote in *God in Search of Man* (p. 296), is "What is right living?" Judaism affirms, he said, that "life is indivisible. The inner sphere is never isolated from outward activities. . . . Right living is like a work of art, the product of a vision and of a wrestling with concrete situations."

The Role of Law in Jewish Ethics

Understandably, the more orthodox a Jewish person is, the more focused he or she will be on legal codes of behavior and their rabbinic interpretations—known in Hebrew as *halakhah,* meaning "the way." The more liberal a Jewish person is, the more he or she will focus on the human dynamics of the communities in which Jewish legal/ethical norms evolved. In economic matters, for example, Orthodox Jews are vastly more influenced by the biblical command not to work on the Sabbath than are liberal Jews.

Yet even Jews who stress the importance of individual conscience in both ritual and ethical matters, and thus do not consider *halakhah* to be binding, nevertheless tend to recognize it as a meaningful expression of the *values* that their people have embraced over the millennia. For any Jew, therefore, regardless of positioning on the orthodox-to-liberal spectrum, it provides a valuable ethical knowledge base.

Sources of Legal Authority

Just as American jurists have the Federal and State Constitutions to draw on as an initial frame of reference, the rabbis had something resembling a constitution in the Torah, the first five books of the Hebrew Bible. But much of that text related to a priest-led community that had gone out of existence after the destruction of the Second Temple in the year 70 C.E. (Throughout this book, I use the nondenominational notations C.E. and B.C.E., meaning Common Era and Before the Common Era, rather than the Christian-based notations of A.D. and B.C.)

Actually, the role of the temple priesthood had already diminished with the dispersion of the Jewish people to Babylonia and other locales after the destruction of the First Temple in 586 B.C.E. So there had been a six-hundred-year period in which "Torah law" had to be interpreted for life in non-temple, Diaspora communities. This need for interpretation became even more pronounced after the Second Temple was destroyed.

Rabbinic opinions about the applicability of Torah law (as well as the other books of the Hebrew Bible, known collectively as *Tanakh*) to new circumstances are referred to as the "oral law." For many years, the rabbinic understandings were, in fact, transmitted orally. But in the second century C.E., an authoritative written compendium of postbiblical rabbinic laws, called the *Mishnah*, was published. This codification organized the laws according to several categories. Most of them dealt with ritual, but several dealt with commercial issues, including damages, trading, employment, property transfer, and usury.

In view of the fact that the Mishnah is eighteen hundred years old, many of its commercial laws seem very archaic today. Yet some have an amazing relevance to modern times. For example, the Mishnah contains extensive commentary on cases involving what we moderns refer to as contributory negligence. And the Mishnah is remarkably explicit, in a highly patriarchal era, that females may claim damages and are liable for damages.

Nevertheless, the Mishnah's commercial laws do look archaic to modern eyes. Indeed, they seemed outdated even in their own era. So the appearance of the Mishnah did not by any means put an end to rabbinic legal commentary and interpretation. Its very publication generated additional argumentation that continued, in both written and oral form, for several hundred years. In the sixth century, a vast compilation of rabbinic commentary on both the Torah and the Mishnah was published, known as the *Talmud*.

The literary style of the Talmud is extremely difficult for Western-trained readers. It is a recording of a series of actual and hypothetical monologues and dialogues by noted rabbinic authorities (who often lived decades or even centuries apart from each other), with precise logical analyses seemingly haphazardly interwoven with legendlike homiletics. Despite its difficult literary style, however, the Talmud achieved a stature in Jewish life that virtually paralleled that of the Torah itself. For the rabbis of the talmudic period made a declaration that became normative for Orthodox Jews ever after. They asserted that the oral law was, in effect, as direct a communication from God as the written law of Torah. In modern times, even non-Orthodox Jews, the great majority of whom do not believe that God communicates to mortals in a detailed way, usually assign a remarkable degree of respect to the Talmud's insights into human behavior.

The Talmud provided a new frame of reference for a subsequent outpouring of communal statutes and legal interpretations that lent a distinct flavor to social and economic life, as well as to religious life, in Jewish settlements of the Diaspora. During the Middle Ages, Jewish people lived in largely self-contained and self-governing communities. This situation continued even after the European Enlightenment in many countries that did not grant Jews the status of ordinary citizens.

Thus, for many centuries after the Talmud was published, and throughout the many Western and Eastern lands in which Jews resided, respected rabbis were consulted for guidance in all aspects of life. Beyond mere guidance, moreover, there were rabbinic courts of law that could regulate daily activity via powers of sanction. Among these powers, the threat of ostracism from the community was highly effective because of the hostility that would be encountered by a Jew cast into an alien world.

Central to the post-talmudic outpouring of legal opinion was a magisterial fourteen-volume codification of Jewish law in the late twelfth century by Moses Maimonides. He entitled his work *Mishneh Torah*, meaning "Second Torah," because he hoped that it would offer the Jewish world so comprehensive a compendium that no one would have need to search in prior books for guidance. In distinct contrast to the eccentric literary style of the Talmud, the *Mishneh Torah* is written in precise Aristotelian style, much like that of Thomas Aquinas, who drew on the same philosophic tradition.

Maimonides' opinions about Jewish ethics have relevance to many issues of modern commerce. For example, a perennial question in marketing is where to draw the line between gilding the lily and being downright misleading. Maimonides addressed that issue in a very realistic way when he wrote (*Sales* 18.2) that a merchant "should not deck out . . . old vessels so that they appear new, but he may deck out the new ones by polishing, ironing, or beautifying them all they require." This dictum leaves room for interpretation, but it establishes a pretty good standard for further discussion.

Notwithstanding Maimonides' desire to be the final authority, differences of rabbinic opinion were pervasive as the life circumstances of Jews continued to change. These differences can be seen in an examination of the so-called *Responsa* literature, compendiums of rabbinic answers to questions posed to them. For example, one rabbi might consider it praiseworthy for a Jew to donate money to a Christian church, while another might consider it a sacrilege. To their great credit, however, the rabbis held minority opinions in high regard because they recognized that a minority opinion under certain circumstances could become a majority opinion under other circumstances.

While the rabbis were, and continue to be, central to the evolution of Jewish law, it is important to note that they gave great weight to the local customs of each community. In some respects, community opinion seemed to lead rather than follow rabbinic legal opinion. Often the role of the rabbis was not so much to initiate behavioral norms as to assure that local customs did not distort or negate the religious or moral demands of Judaism. Highlighting the important role of communal customs is the fact that lay leaders of towns often sat as members of tribunals, especially in arbitration cases. This helped to keep the evolution of Jewish jurisprudence grounded in practical life situations.

Balancing Efficiency and Equity

Jewish civil law has not officially regulated any sizable community in recent times. Even in Israel most civil law (other than on quasi-religious matters such as marriage and divorce) is based on British common law, not religious law. Nevertheless, the earlier two-thousand-year history of law and communal custom can hardly be considered irrelevant to anyone seeking insight into Jewish perspectives on commercial ethics. In part III, I will show how this history—as well as the history of other religious traditions—can inform discussions of specific cases in the modern global marketplace. It will be apparent, I think, that Jewish commercial ethics reflects a careful balancing of pragmatism and idealism, of efficiency and equity.

This balancing effort shows up in many ways. For example, shrewd bargaining has always been permissible and expected, but this does not excuse buyers or sellers for withholding vital information that the other cannot obtain in a normal due diligence investigation. It would not be an exaggeration to say that the Security and Exchange Commission's rules against trading on inside information had their counterpart in the Talmud fifteen hundred years ago.

Likewise in the workplace, modern collective bargaining rules and regulations have antecedents in Jewish history. Jews have always expected employers and employees to bargain the terms of employment. But basic human values may not be bargained away, and strong efforts should be made to prevent either party from exercising coercive powers against the other. Similarly in community affairs, the Jewish history of environmental regulation reveals a careful effort to balance the property rights of individuals against the needs of society as a whole.

New Testament Ethics

Do your own business and work with your own hands, that you may walk honestly toward those who are without and that you may lack nothing.

When I first read these words of Saint Paul (from his First Letter to the Thessalonians 4:11-12), I was rather surprised by their homespun quality. I had always thought of Paul as the first theologian of Christianity. So when I began to do some serious reading of the New Testament, I expected his letters to be filled with ethereal words revolving around the life, death, and resurrection of Jesus. While Paul's theological concerns were certainly reflected in his letters, I was startled to learn that he also was responding to many down-to-earth questions raised by members of early Christian congregations.

Not least among these questions was how the followers of Jesus should behave in the marketplace. In his answers, Paul condemned laziness, deceptive commercial practices, and individuals who put their own interests above those of the community. Moreover, as I dug deeper into the New Testament, it seemed to me that the Gospels also contained ethical messages for Christians in the marketplace that are relevant even in modern times. These included messages about the responsible use of wealth and the importance of reciprocity in relationships between employers and employees.

I realized, however, that I was reading the New Testament through the lenses of a pro-capitalist Jewish businessman. I recognized that Christians and anticapitalists might read the text differently. Moreover, as I probed further I discovered that Roman Catholics and Protestants often read scripture differently from each other, as well as from the way I might read it. (I have not studied the Orthodox branches of the faith but hope to do so one day.)

The Many Ways of Reading the New Testament

As the saying goes, even the devil can quote scripture. If so, then surely people of goodwill can have different understandings of New Testament ethics. A preacher who is politically liberal, for example, will likely have a very different interpretation of the golden rule than his counterpart, even of the same denomination, who is politically conservative.

Differences of New Testament interpretation lie not only in the different political, economic, or sociological views of the interpreters. They lie in the very fabric of the text. The tone of John's Gospel, for example, is quite different from that of the Synoptic Gospels. Even the portrayal of Jesus is different—ethereal and surrounded in mystery according to John, but much earthier according to Matthew, Mark, and Luke. And the letters of Paul oscillate continuously between Paul the theologian and Paul the pastoral counselor.

Consider as well the stark differences between the socioeconomic climate of Jesus' day and our own as a source of interpretive differences. When Jesus lived, most of the population barely eked out a living from family farming of subsistence plots or from working for a small number of wealthy landowners. References to the poor in the New Testament were statements about social misfortune as well as meager material resources. The poor were people with physical handicaps, orphans, or widows without sons to support them and give them dignity. They were people without social standing as well as without economic means. In contrast, "rich" people were those who had a stable place in society—land, a family, and social respectability. To the extent that they had much more than most, it was generally presumed that the excess was garnered by taking advantage of others.

Clearly, the socioeconomic context of the New Testament was strikingly different from the present. Except in underdeveloped areas of the world, most populations are not rural at present, and life expectancy is triple to quadruple what it was then. Most people in the developed world do not have wealth or servants, yet most are not poor. Moreover, economic rewards to all factors of production in market-oriented economies—land, labor, capital, and entrepreneurship—are assumed, in general, to reflect value added to society. One person's gain is not usually thought to reflect another's loss.

Given these vast differences between the society of Jesus' day and our own, it should not be surprising that different people can all be deeply believing Christians yet draw different moral messages from the same scripture. Some Christians read the New Testament in an "eschatological" context. They focus heavily on the text's promise of a world to come, when Christ will return and humanity will dwell in the kingdom of God. To them, the text is not about the practical affairs of everyday life here and now.

Other readers see in the text a call to remake the world as a prelude to the final days. They recognize the great differences in the societal conditions of our day from those of Jesus, but they know there also are some striking similarities. Although most people in developed societies do not lead marginal lives, either economically or socially, many still do; and many more do in less economically developed areas of the world. Moreover, even many well-to-do families are broken by drugs and violence. This is the "liberationist" perspective on the New Testament, which insists that life here and now, with all of its competitiveness, inequities, and inequalities, should not be that way. It sees in the New Testament a demand for radical change.

Still other readers accept the promise of a Second Coming yet try to find in the text as many guides as possible about how to live the best possible life in the society we have. This way of reading the New Testament tends to see Christ's unconditional love more as an ideal model to which the faithful should aspire than one that can be closely followed in a competitive secular world. In such a world, the challenge is to reconcile the ideal with practical accommodations to everyday events. This is the approach I think most Christians have taken—whether Catholic or Protestant—but they have not gotten there in quite the same way.

Scripture versus Reason

Catholic ethicists usually begin their pursuit of moral understanding by trying to discern "the laws of nature." Then they turn to scripture for verification or amendment of what their natural law reasoning has suggested. Protestant ethicists, in contrast, more often begin with scripture and then move toward reasoning. That is, they first look for the moral teachings conveyed by scriptural passages. Then, if the right kind of behavior is not clear from the text, they examine the context of the scriptural passages and reason their way toward moral conclusions.

James Gustafson, in a book entitled *Protestant and Roman Catholic Ethics*, has tried to explain the Protestant emphasis on scripture. "According to most Protestants," he says (p. 20), "God 'published' the law because humanity is shrouded in such darkness that we hardly begin to grasp natural law [through our reasoning powers.]" Human reasoning, in this view, is so likely to be filtered through individual personal experiences and prejudices—along with a basically sinful nature—that it is necessary to turn primarily to scriptural revelation of God's word as the source of ethical understanding.

Ironically, Catholics take the same argument about the influence of subjective factors on human reasoning and reach an opposite conclusion. In their view, the very choice of scriptural passages on which to focus is likely to reflect the predispositions of the person reading scripture. Therefore, they argue, it is more objective to reason about natural law *before* turning to scripture. Indeed, Pope John Paul II has observed that this approach may be particularly appropriate in a global society, because it can seek support from the wisdom of many different cultures.

For example, a major theme of both Catholic and Protestant ethics is the importance of maintaining the human dignity of workers. Yet it is striking that M. Douglas Meeks, a Protestant theologian, uses almost fifty biblical citations to make the point in his book *God the Economist*, double the number used by Pope Leo XIII in *Rerum Novarum*, the first major encyclical on the rights of labor. Moreover, the pope discusses the *reasonableness* of his arguments at length, showing how his interpretations of scripture are in accord with natural law. This effort to meld both faith and reason would be alien to most Protestants. For them, it was quite strange that Pope John Paul II felt it necessary, in 1998, to issue an entire encyclical on the subject, called *Fides et Ratio: On the Relationship between Faith and Reason.*

Autonomy versus Hierarchy

Paralleling their different attitudes about the role of scripture versus natural law and logical reasoning, Catholics and Protestants have differed greatly in their attitudes about who is best able to understand how the word of God should be applied by Christians. In his book *The Making of Moral Theology: A Study of the Roman Catholic Tradition*, John Mahoney says that the Latin word *magisterium*, while supposedly connoting a rather broad church teaching authority, has tended to be restricted in practice to the teaching of the church's hierarchy. It has been used to convey a sense that when a member of the hierarchy teaches, he does so as "a *magister*, or a greater person in charge of anything, as contrasted with a *minister*, or lesser person" (p. 116).

It was exactly this attitude that Martin Luther and the Protestant Reformers condemned. Protestants have claimed not only that the basic information necessary to lead a good Christian life is all in the Bible, but that most people imbued with the Holy Spirit have the capacity to read it and understand its meaning for their lives. In the Protestant view, the Catholic *magisterium* places a barrier between the people and God.

These methodological and ideological differences between Catholics and Protestants are reflected in the ways they each approach the subject of economic ethics. I need to elaborate on that here, in order for the case material in part III to be most meaningful.

Teachings of Popes and Bishops

The Catholic Church's dissemination of its moral messages begins with papal encyclicals. They set an overall tone that bishops, and ultimately parish priests, adapt to regional and local conditions. While the church had always taught the need for social compassion, especially generosity to the poor, *Rerum Novarum,* issued in 1891, asserted that social justice lies at the heart of Christian ethics. The encyclical was written at a time of violent clashes between aggressive captains of industry and socialist revolutionaries. Pope Leo XIII took a firm stand against socialism and in favor of private property rights, but he made it clear that property rights entail important responsibilities, especially to workers. While he did not explicitly endorse the right of labor unions to strike, he was emphatic about the needs of labor for decent pay and working conditions—needs that not only businesses but also government must recognize and support.

Rerum Novarum presented themes that subsequent pontiffs built on, most notably in three encyclicals that celebrated its fortieth, seventieth, and one hundredth anniversaries. In 1931, the world was mired in a catastrophic economic depression and there were many proposals for massive government action. Pope Pius XI, in *Quadragesimo Anno*, advocated a "principle of subsidiarity," by which he meant that government should not do what individuals can do for themselves, and national governments should not do what local governments can do better. He did not deny an important role to national—or even transnational—government agencies, but he warned against governments that overpower grass-roots efforts to achieve individual and family fulfillment.

By 1961, the ruins of the Second World War had led to a vast global economic expansion. Pope John XXIII and his advisers were confident that government and industry could practice their respective specialties in a balanced manner that would sustain and spread the prosperity. Thus, in *Mater et Magistra*, this pope took a much more benign view of governmental action to achieve social goals than his predecessors had. In particular, he called on the governments of highly developed nations, and on organizations such as the United Nations, to focus some of their energies on improving conditions in the underdeveloped regions of the world.

While Pope John's broadening of the church concerns for social justice continued after 1961, his encyclical's reputed "opening to the left" did not. On the hundredth anniversary of Leo XIII's encyclical, as one after another formerly socialist country adopted democratic capitalism, Pope John Paul II issued *Centesimus Annus*, subtitled "The Economics of Human Freedom." In it, the pope clearly recognized that social justice requires an expanded economic product, not just a more equitable distribution of that product. Moreover, he endorsed free markets as the economic system most likely both to enlarge the pie and to distribute it fairly.

John Paul II did not suggest that a free marketplace should be unregulated by government. He endorsed full employment policies or, at the very least, adequate unemployment insurance programs. However, the pope added to the principle of subsidiarity, which limits the role of the central government, a principle of "solidarity." This means that business managers cannot view social responsibility as only the government's domain. John Paul II acknowledged the legitimate role of profit as an indication that a business is functioning well, but he asserted (in section 35) that profitability is not the only indicator of a firm's condition. "The purpose of a business firm," he said, "is to be found in its very existence as a community of persons . . . at the service of the whole of society."

Two publications by the U.S. Catholic Bishops' Conference illustrate how the next layer of the church hierarchy carries forward the papal encyclicals. In 1986, the bishops issued a huge document entitled *Economic Justice for All.* It pulled together their thoughts about economic matters, with particular emphasis on the politically liberal themes of *Mater et Magistra*, such as workers' rights to full employment. Five years later, however, *Centesimus Annus* was published, with its more pro-business tone. So, in 1996, after much deliberation, the Bishops' Conference released a brief ten-point statement called *Catholic Framework for Economic Life.* While they did not retract the liberal principles of the 1986 document, the bishops added that able-bodied people have a *responsibility* to work and contribute to the broader society as well as a *right* to employment and the protection of society.

While the bishops of the church try to add local flavor to the very broad context of papal encyclicals, their publications are also quite general. Consider, for example, the many ethical issues involved in a decision to move production from high-cost to lower-cost locations. Many people would be hurt by such a move, but many others would gain. Suppose that a Catholic businessperson was trying to make such a decision and asked his or her parish priest for advice. Neither the social encyclicals nor the bishops' statements would provide much concrete guidance to the priest.

To help parish priests, Catholic scholars over many years produced so-called moral manuals of much greater specificity. In the past fifty years or so, these manuals have tended to gather dust on most church library shelves. Increasingly, priests and laity want to develop their own ideas about how to apply generalized church teachings to concrete situations. Nevertheless, the manuals provide important insights into Catholic thought about marketplace ethics, and I will draw on them in the case discussions in part III.

And How Do Protestants Decide?

When a Protestant developer of inner-city housing in Chicago was asked to sum up his approach to business ethics, he said that he continuously asks the question: What kind of a homebuilding company would Jesus establish and own? He concluded that Jesus would build durable and resource-efficient homes that satisfy a family's needs rather than its desire for luxuries. In addition, the homes would be laid out in a way that fosters neighborly relationships.

An ethics that begins by asking: What would Jesus do?—which is what WWJD means on T-shirts—comes naturally to a Christian of any denomination. A Catholic can start to look for answers by turning to official church pronouncements, but a Protestant has to be more eclectic and self-reliant. A good place for a Protestant to start is with the views of Reformation leaders.

Martin Luther launched the Protestant Reformation early in the sixteenth century, with an attack on the materialism that he felt had come to pervade Christian life, including the life of the church. He greatly admired the peasants, because he felt they were least touched by the "corroding spirit of commercial calculation." Despite his negative feelings about commercial activity, however, it became necessary for Luther to address the subject. A key to his approach was what he called an ethic of excellence. He said that a Christian cobbler does not make a *Christian* shoe; he makes a *good* shoe. In an article on trade and usury, he acknowledged that merchants need to make a good profit for their "trouble, labor, and risk," but he denounced "wicked tricks" and "sharp practices." He insisted, moreover, that faithful Christian businessmen must control their natural greed and recognize their duties to their fellow men.

John Calvin, twenty-six years younger than Luther, was converted to Protestantism by the forcefulness of Luther's writings. But, whereas Luther's economic mind-set was that of a rural peasant, Calvin worked and thought within the thriving urban commercial and financial environment of Geneva. This difference in life experience probably was an important reason why Calvin was more tolerant than Luther of the accumulation of riches. Indeed, Calvin suggested that the attainment of wealth might be a sign of favor in God's eyes. Yet Calvin was no less contemptuous of greed than Luther. The difference was that where Luther only grudgingly acknowledged that merchants add value to society, Calvin saw business creativity and initiative as vital contributions to the commonweal.

Despite Calvin's exposure to, and sympathy for, commercial activity in his city of Geneva, he could only vaguely sense the coming of the Industrial Revolution. Two hundred years later, John Wesley saw it unfolding before his very eyes. Wesley took to heart the struggles of laborers and farmers that the world's industrialization was bringing about. A sermon entitled "The Use of Money" captures much of his commercial ethic. In it he enunciated "three plain rules": (1) gain all you can (without hurting your neighbor); (2) save all you can (by being thrifty and humble); and (3) give all you can (first to your personal household, then to all of the faithful, and then to all people).

The teachings of these Reformation leaders show non-Catholic Christianity coming to terms with, and developing an ethical response to, the evolving marketplace. In this regard, Protestant thought was more responsive to the pace of modernity than Catholic thought. Recall that the Catholic Church's response did not really come until 1891, with Pope Leo XIII's encyclical *Rerum Novarum*. Yet long before that, Luther, Calvin, and Wesley had preached (with greater or lesser enthusiasm) that the ethics of Christian scripture could be reconciled with the marketplace.

Protestant leaders from the late eighteenth century through much of the nineteenth century focused more on their congregants' inner spiritual lives than on everyday ethics. William Booth's Salvation Army is a well-known example of the many evangelical and revivalist movements that were born during those years. This is not to say that social ethics was absent from the sermons of revivalist preachers. Many spoke out against such social ills as child labor and slavery, for example. Nevertheless, they tended to focus much less on social than on spiritual transformation.

As the twentieth century unfolded, however, the societal upheavals of the Industrial Revolution proceeded with unabated force, and Protestant clerics had to respond. Unlike the revivalists, the new generation of preachers attributed the world's evils not so much to the population's lack of personal spirituality as to perverse political and social structures. Led by Walter Rauschenbusch, pastor of a downtrodden working-class congregation in New York City, they were angry about the inequities of existing institutions but optimistic that a largely Christian population could be convinced that love of neighbor is the supreme ethical principle. They believed that employers, employees, churches, and governments would respond to their pleas for cooperation rather than conflict. They called what they were searching for "the social gospel."

Although the social gospel implied radical change, its proponents insisted that political authority must not infringe on individual liberties. They were optimistic about the possibilities for radical social change without totalitarian authority. Critics argued that this was naively utopian. Reinhold Niebuhr and other advocates of what they called "Christian Realism" stressed that it is a mistake to be very optimistic about the moral perfectibility of human beings. Moreover, they argued, it is a mistake to believe that a highly activist government would not oppressively infringe on individual liberties. Two horrendous world wars, and the evidence of socialist states becoming despotic, gave support to the critics' case.

While the spirit of the social gospel has persisted in a good deal of Protestant moral teaching, a growing number of ministers and lay leaders have taken far less radical positions. As I will show in part III, they are confronting on-the-ground issues of how Christians can be true to their faith while participating fully in the competitive, capitalist marketplace.

Dignity of the Human Person

Clearly, Protestants have differed significantly from Catholics in the ways they extract ethical understandings from the New Testament. And yet, in the final analysis, I believe that each could easily say "Amen" to the other's conclusions. If there is a single theme that could tie those conclusions together, I believe it would be the dignity of the human person. With regard to the marketplace, Catholics and Protestants are in agreement that human dignity is compromised when people deceive each other or treat each other like commodities.

Teachings of the Prophet

German Bank Plans Islamic Stock Fund

With that headline, the *Wall Street Journal* reported that Commerzbank, a leading German financial institution, was planning to establish a new common stock mutual fund that would invest only in equities of companies whose businesses are consonant with Islamic law. This restriction rules out the stocks of companies involved with alcohol, tobacco, pork, gambling, military weapons, or lending money at interest. The latter prohibition presumably would make the stocks of most of the world's banks and insurance companies ineligible—including, ironically, the stock of Commerzbank itself. What is particularly interesting is that the new fund was being aimed not at Muslims living in predominantly Islamic countries, where such funds already exist, but at Muslims living in Germany and other nations where Muslim communities are small but growing rapidly. (Note that the term *Islam* refers to the religion, while *Muslim* is the term for one who is a member of the *Islamic* faith community.)

While there are quite a few so-called social responsibility mutual funds in existence, they have never attracted much money from investors, who usually want their portfolio managers to have a fairly high degree of flexibility. Yet, according to the *Wall Street Journal* article, Commerzbank believes that there are many billions of dollars in the hands of Muslims living in Europe and America who want to feel confident that their money will be invested in accord with their religious ethics.

Sources of Muslim Law and Ethics

Muslims believe that Allah, the one and only God, communicates his wishes through prophets, of whom there have been many, including Moses and Jesus. But Muhammad (who was born around 570 C.E.) was the last and final prophet of Allah in Islamic theology. Muhammad is referred to as "the seal of the prophets."

Muslims view the *Qur'an* (often called, in English, the *Koran*) as a recording of Allah's direct revelations to Muhammad. They were recited orally by the Prophet over a twenty-two-year period, beginning when he was forty years old and ending at the time of his death (around 632 C.E.) Muhammad's recitations were put into written form after his death.

According to the *Qur'an* (15:28-29), the Lord said to the angels: "I am going to create a human being from fermented clay dried tingling hard. And when I have fashioned him and breathed into him of my spirit, bow before him in homage." This striking passage highlights an important Islamic precept. Human beings are thought to be the pinnacle of God's creative energies—higher than the angels, and below only Allah himself. Yet the Qur'anic recitations recognize that this anthropocentrism can lead believers to be arrogant. The danger is resisted in several ways.

First, total submission to Allah is demanded. Second, the *Qur'an* emphasizes that humans are simply *trustees* for Allah of the material world that he created. This trust requires them to develop a moral social order.

The centrality of community—in Arabic, the *umma*—is a third defense against human arrogance. Countless verses of the *Qur'an* assert that the individual Muslim must consider his own needs within the context of the needs of the entire Islamic community. Individual actions that foster a spirit of communal divisiveness are abhorrent.

Finally, Allah does not make it easy for humans to serve as his trustees. They must engage in a constant struggle between their good and their evil inclinations, and they cannot persevere in this struggle without constantly seeking divine guidance. While Allah has given humans the power of reason, the *Qur'an* cautions people not to think that reason alone is a sufficient basis for moral instruction.

Revelation versus Reason

Although Muslims are supposed to make virtuous moral choices, virtue alone does not tell a person how to behave in specific situations. Nor can the *Qur'an* describe all possible circumstances in which a moral choice has to be made. When the Prophet was alive, he could be consulted for situational guidance. After his death, a compilation was published that gave numerous illustrations of how he lived and what he said beyond the Qur'anic recitations. Known as the *Hadith*, or "Traditions of the Prophet," this compilation helped to preserve Muhammad's, and his disciples', situational guidance.

Nevertheless, it was understood that more formal tools had to be developed to respond to continuous changes in the affairs of life. In Islam, the virtuous exercise of human choices requires methods of discerning the details of Allah's law, known as the *shari'a*—which means "the way to the watering hole," a metaphor for "the right path."

During the centuries that followed the Prophet's death, there were great, often divisive, debates in the Muslim world about the proper way to discern the *shari'a*. The debates, which have parallels in both Judaism and Christianity, are a reflection of two fundamentally different mind-sets. One makes human reasoning and natural law primary, utilizing scripture and other revelatory information to confirm reason or to deal with issues that reason cannot cope with. The other sees revelatory information as primary and takes human reason as, at best, a supplement.

Given this conflict, a compromise version of Muslim law became the most widely accepted. Essentially, it takes as eternally authoritative not only scripture but also the independent reasoning of sages who lived through the second century of the Muslim era (i.e., until around 800 C.E.). These men were considered to be divinely inspired because of their close connection in time to the Prophet's life, words, and mode of living.

For situations not contemplated by the early sages, however, reliance would be placed on each succeeding generation's *ulama*. These are the Muslim community's recognized experts in *Qur'an, Hadith,* and the reasoning of the early sages. They use their knowledge to draw analogies from the original sources. By thus combining the independent reasoning of sages who were closest to the Prophet with the reasoning-by-analogy of later scholars, Muslims throughout the world are able to consider the entire *shari'a*, as it has evolved over the centuries, to be divine in origin. (Note the similarity to traditional Judaism and Roman Catholicism, which accord divine status to "oral law"—pronouncements by talmudic rabbis and popes—in addition to "written law," i.e., the Bible.)

Under the umbrella of this legal methodology, there is an important doctrine having to do with community consensus. The *Hadith* reports Muhammad as having said: "My community does not agree on an error." While Muhammad was alive, of course, the community could not be in error because his final word was decisive if there were communal disputes. The *Hadith* indicates, however, that Muhammad did a fair amount of consulting with key members of the community before rendering decisions.

After Muhammad's death, there was a problem, because no single person inherited his binding authority—at least in Sunni Islam, which represents the vast majority of the world's Muslims. As a result, community consensus has generally been understood to refer to consensus opinions of the *ulama*, the recognized Sunni legal experts. (The Muslim minority most well known in the West is the Shi'ite group, who live mainly in Iran. Shi'ites believe that there was a chain of inheritance of Muhammad's authority. Thus, they are more restrictive than Sunni Muslims regarding the people who may act as interpreters, whom they refer to as *ayatullahs.*)

Of course, legal experts often differ with each other. Major Sunni jurists have usually respected each other's opinions; but Muslim lay people may not simply "shop around" for opinions they find convenient. They must select a particular authority and follow his advice consistently.

Perspectives on Private Property and Value Added

Islam teaches that work necessary to support oneself and one's family is as worthy in the eyes of God as the performance of religious duties. Indeed, work is sometimes seen as a religious duty in and of itself. Moreover, whatever work is done, according to the *Hadith,* should be done to perfection.

To be sure, the duty to work and provide for one's needs must be kept in check. The *Qur'an* emphasizes the dangers of greed and covetousness and warns against excessive accumulation of wealth. A traditional Islamic story relates that when Muhammad lay dying, he pointed to the money that he had left and asked how he could face Allah with this wealth in his possession. His wife, A'isha, thereupon proceeded to give the money to charity.

Yet Islamic law recognizes that it is natural for even very philanthropic people to want to leave some of their material wealth to their relatives. A healthy balance is needed. Accordingly, the *Qur'an* and numerous non-

Qur'anic laws go into great detail about how a deceased's wealth should be distributed.

Sayyid Qutb was the leader of one of the most radical strains of Islamic fundamental revivalism in the twentieth century, hence hardly likely to be an apologist for modern economic institutions. Still, he affirms in his book *Social Justice in Islam* (pp. 102–3) that people are "created with a natural love of wealth for its own sake," citing the Qur'anic verse: "Verily the love of wealth is strong." It follows, says Qutb, that competition for personal possessions is natural and in many ways desirable. For it encourages people to do their best at their jobs. He observes that the stern Islamic punishment for theft, cutting off the hand of the thief, indicates the importance of property rights.

While recognizing private property rights, however, Islamic law has developed a strong negative attitude toward private monopolies. These are particularly odious if the products involved represent necessities of life. Clearly, Islamic tradition does not favor a strongly individualistic and unrestricted economic structure. Always, the interests of the individual are supposed to be balanced against the needs of the community.

Concepts of Value Added

Perhaps because of its emphasis on communal needs, Islamic tradition displays a sort of hierarchy of economic values. The production of goods that satisfy basic needs is viewed more positively than the production of luxury items, and the development of natural resources is put on a higher spiritual plane than trade and manufacturing. This is not to say that only the production and processing of natural resources are considered to be socially useful employment. After all, Muhammad himself was a merchant prior to becoming leader of the new religious movement. Indeed, the *Hadith* refers to merchants as being "couriers of the world" and "trusted servants of God upon earth." On the other hand, simply *being* a merchant is not *prima facie* evidence that a person is performing useful service to the community.

An example of a useful act by a middleman would be arranging for distant goods to be brought to the local market. This adds value by making available products that would otherwise not be available. On the other hand, suppose a lessee sublets his leased dwelling place at a markup of rent. This probably would not be considered a value-adding activity unless the lessee had made an improvement to the facility.

Islamic tradition has had a particularly dim view of finance as a value-adding activity. Muslims are not permitted to lend money at fixed rates of interest, and many other types of financial activities, while not necessarily prohibited by Islamic law, are clearly at the lower end of the ladder of occupations considered to be socially useful. Activities that seem to smack of gambling, such as securities trading and insurance businesses, are viewed skeptically; and activities such as "selling short"—that is, selling borrowed assets in the expectation that their price will fall—is almost surely illegal in the opinion of Islamic jurists.

The Bazaar, the Community, and the Mosque

Islam views the marketplace not simply as an economic venue but as a spiritual venue as well. Roy Mottahedeh, author of *The Mantle of the Prophet*, sums it up in an interesting way. When two people happen to meet on the street, he says (pp. 34–35), they meet each other simply as two people. But when they meet in the marketplace, they encounter each other in a special way. The bazaar, he says, has been recognized for over a thousand years as a special arena of Islamic life. In this arena, people share certain moral obligations. "Not only prices but men's reputations are set, reset, and continually adjusted in the bazaar." Thus, says Mottahedeh, "the bazaar and the mosque are the two lungs" of Islamic communal life.

Verse 49:9 of the *Qur'an* says: "If two groups of believers come to fight one another, promote peace between them." Therefore, when an Islamic jurist confronts a dispute over the meaning of the terms of a commercial agreement, he usually urges that it be submitted to arbitration in the interests of communal harmony. Islam recognizes the right of mature individuals to enter into formal and informal agreements that determine their economic relationships. Yet it insists that a network of individual relationships must contribute to a healthy *umma*.

4

Wisdom Traditions of the East

Business as an Ashram: Hindu Reflections

A twofold path has been taught by Me;
the path of knowledge for men of discrimination
and the path of works for men of action.

This verse is from the *Bhagavad Gita,* one of the most revered documents in Hindu sacred scriptures. It suggests that there are two ways for a person to live. One, the "path of knowledge," is a path of detachment. The other, the "path of works," is a path of action. Most Hindus hesitate to choose one or the other path exclusively; they try to walk both and their effort is reflected in the marketplace.

There are several reasons to study this aspect of Hindu life. First, the sheer number of Hindus is enormous. Most of the billion people who live in India, or who live elsewhere but come from there, are Hindus. Second is the fact that they are playing a growing role in the global economy, particularly in electronics, where India has been developing its own version of Silicon Valley. Third, Buddhism stems from Hinduism; and Buddhism has penetrated all of East Asia and, increasingly, non-Asian parts of the world. Thus, anyone involved in the global marketplace will inevitably confront the ethical attitudes of Hinduism—either directly, or indirectly via the Hindu influence on Buddhism.

To begin our look at these attitudes, I want to paraphrase a story told in a book called *Ethics in Management: Vedantic Perspectives,* by S. K. Chakraborty, an Indian professor of management. He was presiding over a seminar of businessmen in his country, and he asked them to offer their thoughts about the ideal business environment. They developed the following list (p. 26): simplicity, efficiency, frugality, decorum, quality output, customer is God, straightforwardness, brotherhood, self-restraint, punctuality, sharing, trust, humility, care, patience, honesty.

The professor asked them whether they saw any overriding theme in this list. Somewhat to his and their surprise, the consensus of the businessmen was that the quality of work life they had described resembled that of an *ashram*. They were surprised, because an *ashram* is traditionally a place of retreat from the world. Yet it appeared that many of the characteristics of an *ashram* had been transferred to a commercial context as they thought about the ideal business environment. They had conceived of a *business ashram* that bridged the paths of detachment and worldly action. In Chakraborty's view, their metaphor reflected "the ingrained Indian ethos most of our managers secretly nurse."

It was not immediately obvious how the metaphor of a *business ashram* could be made more concrete. So the discussion continued, and the following suggestions emerged: truthful sales practices, efforts to use local resources as much as possible, protection of the environment, and mutual respect between employers and employees. An American reading this list might well be puzzled. If protection of the environment is a priority for these businessmen, why is it that the Indian government resists efforts to establish international trade standards that include environmental protection? And if mutual respect between employers and employees is important, why is there such widespread use of child labor in India? So how does the "ingrained Indian ethos"—to use the professor's words—shed light on these questions?

Hindu Modes of Religious Expression

"Hindu" and "Hinduism" are not terms of Indian origin. They are basically Western terms that encompass a wide variety of religious beliefs and practices that originated on the Indian subcontinent at least 3,500 years ago and continue to the present time. These beliefs and practices are not associated with any single founding personality.

Hinduism is polytheistic, but it also has a monotheistic aspect. Each person chooses a particular god for special devotion, while acknowledging the existence of other gods. For example, a person may be especially devoted to Brahma, the creator god; or to Vishnu, the preserver god; or to Sakti, the divine manifestation of feminism. These gods and others, such as Siva, the god of destruction, are symbolic of one "Brahman," or ultimate reality. The concept has been likened to a single strand of pearls, with each god representing one pearl, or one aspect of divinity. Each Hindu may choose a particular pearl for special treasuring, special honor, and devotion.

Diana Eck, a Christian student of Hindu traditions, has suggested in her book *Encountering God* that the chosen god idea may not be as different from the Abrahamic traditions as it appears on the surface. True, the Abrahamic traditions see God as choosing humans rather than the other way around. Yet, Eck wonders, is it not the case that each individual Jew, Christian, or Muslim has his or her own particular ideas about the characteristics of God that are most meaningful to that person, and which that person chooses to emphasize in developing his or her worldview?

From a Hindu perspective, Eck observes (p. 60), "oneness and manyness are not seen as true opposites." For "if something is important, it is important enough to be repeated, duplicated, and seen from many angles." The Hindu sacred scriptures frequently remind readers that *truth is one, and the wise will call it by many names.*

Since each Hindu is basically free, within broad boundaries, to fashion his or her own way of expressing religious feelings, there is a broad spectrum of practice. It ranges from an intensive inner development of techniques of ego suppression to a very outwardly focused service to others.

Arvind Sharma uses the metaphor of a motion picture to illustrate the idea behind ego suppression. If the drama of life is likened to a movie, he says, Hinduism asserts that humanity is really like the screen. But instead of seeing themselves as parts of the screen, the place on which life's events are projected, individuals wrongly identify themselves with the characters of the movie. Therefore, Hindus who want to truly link themselves with the cosmic drama need to obliterate their sense of self-importance. Consequently, this mode of Hindu religious expression centers on a variety of mental and physical techniques of ego suppression, such as yoga.

The other end of the Hindu spectrum of religious expression is reflected in the life of Mahatma Gandhi. It is characterized by broad ecumenism, absolute nonviolence, and self-sacrificing social service. Most Hindus live their lives somewhere in between these two ends of the spectrum, trying to negotiate as best they can the paths of detachment and action.

Karma, Dharma, and Caste

Regardless of the specific mode of religious expression, all forms of Hinduism have in common the idea of a continuous cycle of birth, death, and rebirth. A major component of this view is that human beings undergo a long-term series of reincarnations, with new incarnations reflecting the moral qualities exhibited in previous incarnations. This is the doctrine known as *karma*.

While some may see a sort of dreariness in the karmic process of reincarnation, it can also be seen as a continuous series of opportunities to improve one's lot by good moral behavior. Westerners so often focus on the mystical aspects of Hinduism that they overlook *karma*'s moral underpinning. *Karma* is not simply a person's destiny; it is a doctrine of rewards and punishments.

Karmic rewards and punishments are not meted out by God, as in Abrahamic traditions, but are imposed by a natural law akin to the physical law of gravity. The moral quality of a person's actions is inevitably manifested in the pleasure or suffering of the others to whom that person relates, and in the pleasure or suffering of the person himself. Moral action is rewarded or punished—if not in one's present incarnation, then in future incarnations.

Beyond this overarching karmic principle, Hinduism asserts that there are four valid goals in the life of any human being: (1) to be moral (*dharma*); (2) to earn a good livelihood (*artha*); (3) to enjoy sensual pleasures (*kama*); and, (4) ultimately, to be liberated from worldly concerns (*moksa*).

Although I've related the word *dharma* to *morality*, it actually is used by Hindus to refer to a wide variety of concepts. These include ultimate cosmic realities, religious and social obligations, righteousness, and justice. The term, *dharma*, is so expansive that it relates not only to general religious and ethical aspects of life, but also to attitudes appropriate to an individual's particular place in the social order and to his particular stage of mental and spiritual development.

Hindu tradition thinks of life as having four stages, each ideally spanning twenty-five years. In one's youth, the first quarter of life, a person should learn the basic principles of morality and of practical economics.

Maturity, the second quarter of life, is involved mainly in raising a family, accumulating material possessions through one's employment, and enjoying the sensual pleasures of life—all within the boundaries, however, of the moral principles learned earlier. As one ages, in the third quarter of life, attention should shift to piety, preferably in a monastic setting. Success in this stage will lead to the last stage, in which one seeks ultimate liberation.

The class, or caste, into which a person is born conditions the specific nature of the life-cycle stages. It is part of one's *dharma*. There are five broad groupings of Hindus that constitute a social hierarchy which is key to interpersonal relationships, especially in rural settings. (Some observers say that caste consciousness tends to be suspended on the "shop floor" in modern India, at least in larger enterprises as opposed to rural farms and cottage industries.)

At the top of the hierarchy is a *Brahman* caste, consisting of priests, intellectuals, and teachers. The function of *brahmans* is to provide society's sense of direction. Next is a caste called *kshatriyas*, which consists of rulers, warriors, and public officials. The function of this caste is to provide the society with orderly administration and protection. Third are the *vaishyas*—farmers, merchants, and financiers—who are in charge of the processes that provide society with its material needs. These three highest castes constitute some 15 percent of India's current population.

Another 50 percent of the population, *shudras*, are the working-class people who get society's necessary jobs done. In this fourth caste, there are subcastes related to specific occupation or residential locale. There is, finally, a casteless group of Hindus, the so-called untouchables. These people are deemed to be ritually impure, a status evidenced by the jobs they do, such as latrine cleaning. They comprise about 20 percent of the population. The remaining 15 percent of Indians are non-Hindus, mainly Muslims.

Hindu tradition does not provide a mechanism whereby a man can, within his lifetime, move from one caste to another (there is some chance for a woman to "marry up"). Indeed, a laborer may become wealthy or learned, yet he remains in the *shudra* caste into which he was born. Likewise, one born a *Brahman* can become an office worker as readily as a priest, yet remain a *Brahman*. Therefore, leading an ethical life obliges one to follow one's socioreligious duties as a member of a particular caste in each stage of one's life. This obligation is highlighted in some of the most widely read portions of the Hindu sacred scriptures.

Hindu Scriptures

The Hindu scriptures are enormous, more than ten times the size of the Bible. The most ancient and authoritative are the Vedas, which are believed to have been revealed supernaturally—referred to as *sruti*. The most cherished part of the Vedas is the final portion, the *Upanishads* (also referred to as Vedanta, meaning end of the Veda). The *Upanishads* describe the gods in both very abstract and very human terms and, importantly, contain the first clear enunciation of the idea of a reincarnation based on the moral quality of one's earlier life.

In addition to the *sruti*, which have revelatory status, the Hindu sacred literature includes a vast *smrti*, which are works by acknowledged human authors. These works are theologically less authoritative than the *sruti*, yet they have had more influence on the lives of ordinary people. The flavor of this influence can be tasted by dipping into two of the most revered documents in the Hindu sacred scriptures. They are the *Bhagavad-Gita*, often referred to simply as the *Gita*, and the *Ramayana*. Both deal with the role of leaders in maintaining social order but have broad implications for ordinary people as well.

The Gita and the Ramayana

Bhagavad-Gita means "Song of the Lord" or "Song of the Beloved One." It has two central characters. One is a high-ranking warrior named Arjuna. The other is Krishna, who is portrayed in the poem as Arjuna's charioteer, but who actually is a human manifestation of the god Vishnu and is a classic spiritual teacher.

Arjuna is preparing to lead a military campaign against an opposing army of his cousins. He is torn by thoughts that it is morally wrong to kill one's own kinsmen, even in war. He asks Krishna for advice, and Krishna's lengthy answer forms the core of the text. It includes the following statements, the first being the one I used to introduce this chapter.

> A twofold path has been taught by Me; the path of knowledge for men of discrimination and the path of works for men of action. (III:3)
>
> Perform the work that has to be done without attachment. . . . [but] perform action also with regard for the maintenance of the world. (III:19–20)

> A man obtains perfection by being devoted to his own proper action. . . . Better is one's own dharma, though imperfect, than the dharma of another, well performed. One does not incur sin when doing the action prescribed by one's own nature. (XVIII:45–47)

These passages reveal the tension in Hindu thinking that I have been stressing. Krishna teaches Arjuna that there are two different ways to live a good life. Both involve discipline; but one (knowledge) refers to disciplined *inactivity*, while the other (works) refers to disciplined *activity*.

By citing inactivity as the way of "men of discrimination," Krishna seems to be favoring it as the better way of life. Indeed, in various other verses he commends it even to the extent of ascetic withdrawal from the world. However, on the whole, as Dominic Goodall puts it in the Introduction of his anthology *Hindu Scriptures* (pp. xiv-xv), "Krishna is much more emphatic in his recommendation of dispassionate action." By "dispassionate action," Goodall means doing what one's station in life demands, and doing it for its own sake rather than for tangible reward.

Of course, Arjuna's question to Krishna was asked in a specific context. He was asking about the morality of leading a battle against his kinsmen. For many centuries, commentaries on the *Gita* focused on the question in that context. They pitted the responsibilities of leadership—being actively involved in the world and leading others to action—against the spiritual ideal of renunciation and ritual observance. In modern times, however, Arjuna's doubts and Krishna's advice have been seen by many as metaphors for a challenge confronting any Hindu believer, not just society's leaders. The challenge is how to reconcile one's *dharma*, or outward worldly responsibilities, with one's inner spiritual path.

The tension between worldly *dharma* and an ideal of renunciation shows up boldly in a Hindu classic that is even more widely read than the *Gita* and is discussed by the Hindu man-in-the-street as well as by scholars. It is the *Ramayana*, meaning "The Travels of Rama." The full work consists of twenty-four thousand Sanskrit verses, which ordinary people cannot be expected to read in entirety. Hence, it has been retold in a variety of shorter books, oral presentations, dances, puppet shows, and the like.

In the *Gita*, Vishnu's incarnation appears as a wise servant, a charioteer named Krishna who gives ethical advice to a community leader, Arjuna. But in the *Ramayana*, the incarnation of Vishnu, who is named Rama, is himself a member of the community's leadership. Rama is a prince, the heir to an important throne. In this work, the ethical advice comes from observing Rama's behavior when he is challenged by a variety of plots against him and his loved ones.

Rama's behavior exhibits two important but contrasting features. On the one hand, he recognizes the status to which he was born, and he adheres steadfastly to his duties as a leader. At the same time, however, he makes it clear that he would prefer a life of contemplation and simplicity. Thus, the message received from the story by most Hindus is a combination of activity and passivity. The message is that one must be active in the world, but with humility and patience.

Humility and Patience in Economic Life

As I think about these Hindu attitudes, I am reminded of people who play cards well. A good card player tries to do the best he can with the hand he is dealt. He doesn't feel entitled to a better hand, and he doesn't spend a lot of energy wishing for a better hand. Nor does he try to win by cheating. He simply does the best he can with the resources he has available at the moment.

Perhaps this is what the professor had in mind when he spoke of "the ingrained Indian ethos" that his audience of business managers "secretly nursed" and that led them to view an *ashram* as the metaphor for an ideal business setting. It would be a setting in which people change for the better that which is capable of change but humbly and patiently accept what cannot be changed right now. In this sense, it provides an answer to my starting questions about environmental and child labor standards in India. It would appear that their Hindu tradition leads the people of India to think of environmental pollution and child labor as evils they simply have to tolerate, for the time being, as a cost of economic development. They hope that things will be better in the future, but their focus is on doing the best they can right now.

Buddhist Insights

***Ethics is the indispensable interface
between my desire to be happy and yours.***

The Dalai Lama wrote these words in a recent book called *Ethics for the New Millennium* (p. 47). His emphasis on happiness—his own, yours, and mine—is somewhat surprising. It seems to clash with another, perhaps better known, aspect of Buddhist thought, namely, that life is ephemeral and that cravings for temporal happiness are ultimately futile. Consider, for example, the following verse from the most widely read collection of the sayings of the Buddha: "When a man considers this world as a bubble of froth . . . the king of death has no power over him" (*Dhammapada* 13:170).

How can the Dalai Lama, probably the modern world's most well known Buddhist, seem to embrace an ethic of happiness when classic Buddhist thinking says that life is a bubble of froth? It is a paradox—reminiscent of the Hindu paradox of activity and detachment. But just as Hindus accept paradox as an inevitable aspect of life and try to find ways of bridging it in their daily activity, so too do Buddhists. Indeed, Buddhism is a tree that grew from the roots of Hinduism.

The Hindu Roots and the Buddhist Tree

Around 500 B.C.E., a man named Gotama was born in India. When people speak of "Buddha" or "the Buddha," they are speaking of that man. Gotama's everlasting contribution to civilization was a refashioning of Hindu ways of encountering the world. He retained the Hindu roots but created a new tree from those roots.

Gotama was comfortable with the Hindu view of life as a *karmic* cycle of birth, death, and rebirth. But he was not content with the traditional attitude that liberation from this cycle is simply a *possibility*. He wanted to find a way of life that might actually achieve it. The liberated state is called *Nirvana*.

Gotama also was uncomfortable with the panoply of god figures in Hindu tradition. He acknowledged the existence of supernatural beings, but he envisioned them more like what Western religions have called angels. They are beings who performed exceptionally virtuous acts in their past corporeal lives and now exist in a sort of heavenly realm. They are beings who are central to the funeral rites of passage that Gotama, and the monks he trained as his disciples, fashioned from their Hindu heritage.

Essentially, Gotama rejected the metaphysical aspects of either a single (Abrahamic-type) God or of the multiple Hindu gods. Yet, while rejecting god figures, the Buddha embraced the moral attributes that we of the West usually ascribe to God. Indeed, he embraced the idea of divine moral attributes even more strongly than did his god-fearing Hindu forebears. At the time Gotama was teaching in India, the caste system was fully developed. A person's social position and all that accompanied such position, including wealth and education, was determined by his birth lineage. The Buddha rejected the concept of privilege through birth and preached a doctrine of nobility through moral conduct and quest for knowledge. Let's examine the nature of that quest.

The Four Noble Truths

The Buddha's teaching, like the wisdom of so many ancient sages, was transmitted orally for a long time. It was finally committed to writing in approximately 50 B.C.E., some four centuries after his death, in a body of work known in Sanskrit as the *Tripitaka* (*Tipitaka* in the Pali language). It means the "Three Baskets," so named because it contains three types of material: sermons of the Buddha, monastic rules of discipline, and a variety of scholarly treatises.

In his first sermon, the Buddha expounded four ideas that have resonated for more than two thousand years. The impact of that sermon was so strong that its commemoration is a major Buddhist religious occasion, and the place where it was delivered and its location—near Banaras, India—is considered sacred space. At the risk of oversimplifying, I offer the following summary of the Buddha's four seminal ideas, known as "the four noble truths."

The Truth of Suffering

Life is characterized by *dukkha*, a word most often translated as *suffering*. *Dukkha* includes aspects of life that almost anyone would relate to suffering—sickness, pain, sorrow, and despair. But the Buddha observed that not getting what one wants is also *dukkha*.

The Buddha did not think that life consists *only* of unrelieved suffering. He was a man who had experimented with many different lifestyles, and he understood that life has many joys. But he had come to understand that happiness is very transitory and that, in their heart of hearts, most people recognize its fleeting nature. The Buddha had the insight to know that this awareness of the fleeting nature of happiness leaves people with a sense of anguish, hence of *dukkha*.

The Truth of Arising

Why does life contain so much *dukkha*? Because, the Buddha said, people have insatiable desires, endless cravings for sensual and material things and experiences. Damien Keown, in his *Very Short Introduction to Buddhism*, suggests an interesting metaphor for the relationship between desire and suffering. He writes (p. 51): "craving fuels suffering in the way that wood fuels a fire [which] consumes what it feeds on without being satisfied. It spreads rapidly, becomes attached to new objects, and burns with the pain of unassuaged longing."

The Truth of Cessation

Since craving is the fuel of suffering, then the extinction of craving is the key to an end of suffering and attainment of the profound inner peacefulness of *Nirvana*. This does not require that desire for the necessities of human existence be extinguished. It does require a person to escape from the all-too-common endless round of one desire leading to another.

The Truth of the Path

How can a person try to make this escape? The Buddha prescribed a "Noble Eightfold Path" to that end. It consists of eight "right" attitudes grouped, in Buddhist tradition, into three categories. All are to be cultivated concurrently and continuously. They are:

Wisdom (*panna*), which includes: (1) right understanding (meaning knowledge and acceptance of the Buddha's teachings), and (2) right resolve (serious commitment to self-transformation).

Morality (*sila*), which includes: (3) right speech (language that is honest, thoughtful, and sensitive), (4) right action (helping others; not killing, stealing, fornicating, etc.), and (5) right livelihood (one that causes no harm to others).

Meditation (*samadhi*), which includes: (6) right effort (a positive, energetic will to rid the mind of unwholesome thoughts and fill it with wholesome thoughts); (7) right mindfulness (keen awareness of how bodily activities and mental feelings arise and disappear); and (8) right concentration (techniques of becoming calm and focusing one's attention on ultimate realities rather than the self).

These eight attitudes constitute a "middle way." The Buddha called it a way that is neither indulgence nor austerity. He made a point of saying that he himself had tried both extremes and found neither to be satisfying. In many ways, it is similar to Aristotle's Golden Mean, although there is no evidence of any contact between the Greek and Indian philosophers of that time.

Everyday Ethics along the Path to Enlightenment

Of the three groups of "right attitudes," *sila* is the one most clearly related to worldly ethics. It consists of right speech, right action, and right livelihood. But it is important also to see that *panna*, or wisdom, connotes an understanding of Buddha's total teaching. Since a most important component of that teaching is compassion for all living things, *panna* as well as *sila* relates to everyday ethics. The third group of right attitudes, *samadhi*, or meditation, is less directly connected to ethics but is not entirely unrelated. Properly practiced, it brings an inner calm that permits a person to speak and act with wisdom and compassion.

Underlying the interrelatedness of *pana, sila,* and *samadhi* is a Buddhist doctrine that has an exotic name in the Pali language—*paticcasamuppada.* It has been translated into English as "dependent origination" or, less formally, as interdependence. It means that every effect has a cause; everything that is or happens originates through some other thing or occurrence. Therefore, as Damien Keown puts it (p. 54), the universe must be seen "not as a collection of more or less static objects but as a dynamic network of interrelated causes and effects."

This view of the universe has important implications for leading an ethical life here and now. Since everything is interrelated, every action of an individual human being has consequences for everything and everyone else, as well as for the individual actor. Good actions have good consequences and bad actions bad consequences—for everything and everyone, whether immediately or at a later time. That understanding has clearly guided the moral life of the Dalai Lama. Because of "the fundamental interconnectedness which lies at the heart of reality," he writes (p. 28), "your interest is also my interest; and "one of the things which determines whether an act is ethical or not is its effect on others' experience or expectation of happiness."

Westerners often wonder whether all of this might suggest that free will is an illusion. After all, reincarnation and interdependence mean that the nature of a person's present life is affected by the nature of prior lives that he did not choose, and by constantly changing events that he cannot influence. Does free will have much meaning in this context?

The Buddha must have known that the question of free will would come up, because he addressed it in his final sermon. In it he told his followers quite emphatically to depend on themselves to find the truths that will enlighten them. He told them to depend on themselves here and now—not on previous lives, not on gods, and not on random chance. It is true, he said, that we cannot control the things that occur to us, but we can control how we respond to them. We can choose right from wrong behavior and, thus, influence our present as well as our future lives. The guiding motif, he urged, should be compassion.

Compassion and Economic Life

Interestingly, the two major branches of the Buddhist tree, *Theravada* and *Mahayana*, have interpreted that teaching somewhat differently. Theravada stresses the *personal* search for *Nirvana*, whereas in Mahayana Buddhism the goal is not only personal enlightenment but also *helping others* to become enlightened—by teaching, motivating, and setting an example.

Mahayana Buddhists are clearly concerned with perfecting the world. The very name of their movement, *Mahayana*, means "great vehicle," and they often refer sarcastically to *Theravada* Buddhism as *Hinayana*, meaning "small vehicle." While *Theravada* is not unconcerned with humanity in general, its scripture has relatively little commentary on what, in modernity, are described as human rights issues. *Theravadan* tradition emphasizes patience and contentment with one's lot in life, and this has often been interpreted to imply a rather stoic acceptance of injustice. On the other hand, *Mahayana* sources provide ample basis for an activist Buddhist sense of social responsibility. I believe that this view is gaining increasing acceptance.

Whichever branch of the tree individual Buddhists may associate with—indeed, even among Zen Buddhists who focus most heavily on the meditative aspects of the tradition—the dominant ethical theme is one of compassion. From the records of his many sermons, it is apparent that the Buddha did not exhibit great interest in the detailed workings of the marketplace. Yet the Buddhist teaching of compassion, a theme that flows from the understanding that all things are interrelated, is hardly irrelevant to the everyday decisions that we all have to make in the marketplace. It is a theme I will explore further in part III.

The Confucian Way

Caught Between Eras:
China's Factory Workers

On November 18, 1999, a *New York Times* article carried this banner headline. The article, and countless articles like it in newspapers all over the world, reflects one of the most dramatic developments in economic history. As an American-style competitive marketplace sweeps over the globe, it is causing major cultural shocks, especially to Chinese, Japanese, and other East Asian people. The text of the *Times* article begins:

> The middle-aged workers outside the aging Beijing No. 2 textile factory said today that they already knew their days of employment were numbered—that they knew it even before China signed a landmark agreement this week to open its doors wider to global competition.
>
> What worries them now, said the two workers, who stopped for a discreet conversation, is how well the government will support them after they get the inevitable notice from the factory.

The expectation of these workers that the government would support them was only in part a reflection of the communist ideology that they had lived with during most of their lives. It also was a reflection of the Confucian tradition that has been part of East Asian culture for many centuries, having originated in China and then spread far and wide. Although it became amalgamated with other religious traditions—most importantly, Taoism in China, Shinto in Japan, Christianity in Korea, and Buddhism throughout the area—one key element of Confucianism maintained its force. That element relates to relationships between "the ruler and the ruled."

Confucian ideas about the ruler and the ruled apply in many aspects of East Asian life—in relationships between the government and the people, between a father and his children, between an employer and his employees. These relationships are characterized by an ethic of reciprocity. The ruler takes care of the ruled in exchange for the latter's loyalty and devotion. In this context, it is perfectly understandable that the Chinese factory workers' first thought was how the government would support them when they lost their jobs. Clearly, a major cultural shock occurs when this ethical mind-set confronts the rugged individualism of American-style competitive markets.

The Confucian Worldview

In an ancient Chinese story, Confucius said to a group of his disciples: "There is one thread that runs through my doctrines." After he left, the disciples asked the senior member of their group: "What did he mean?" Depending on how one translates the senior member's reply into English, he responded that the thread is *conscientiousness and altruism* or *loyalty and reciprocity*.

In recounting this tale in his *Source Book in Chinese Philosophy* (p. 27), Wing-tsit Chan observes that, despite the senior member's explanation, Confucianists have never fully agreed on what the "one thread" is. There have been numerous opinions over the 2,500 years since Confucius lived (551–479 B.C.E.). But while the exact identity of the one thread may be in dispute, there is general agreement that the Confucian ideal is a harmonious relationship among all things in the universe.

In particular, Confucianism focuses on the way human beings interact with each other. The overall Confucian worldview has often been described with a schematic diagram. It is a series of concentric circles of relationships. Family is in the inner circle, community in the next circle, then nation, earthly world beyond the nation, and the world beyond the earthly world as an outer, unbounded circle.

Historical Development of Confucianism

Confucianism did not begin with Confucius. Rather, he was the foremost teacher and sage in a long line that preceded and followed him, and he is accorded the honor of having his name associated with the entire tradition. Actually, the name "Confucius" is not Chinese. The sage was known as Master K'ung. "Confucius" is a latinized pronunciation of K'ung Fu-tzu, which is the Chinese way of saying Master K'ung. Chinese refer not to "Confucianism," but to "The Way." It has its origin over three thousand years ago.

At that time, the tribal family that had been preeminent in China for many hundreds of years was overthrown, and a transition from a tribal to a feudal society began. Along with the change in social structure the new rulers encouraged a change in religious attitudes. In place of the tribal worship of anthropomorphic gods of nature they propounded a new doctrine called "The Mandate of Heaven," which they used to justify their right to rule.

According to this doctrine, there is a heavenly mandate that makes human destiny dependent on virtuous behavior rather than on the whims of the gods. The new rulers asserted that the prior leaders had forfeited their mandate to rule because they failed in their duties to those they ruled. The mandate had passed to the new rulers, who were more virtuous, but it would stay with them only if they continued to be virtuous.

Thus, what has since come to be known as Confucianism began with a need to define virtue for a ruling class and to develop methods of assuring that the ruling class would, in fact, learn and practice virtue. To be sure, spiritual beings were still considered to reside in a heavenly abode and were honored and served as inspirational examples to earthly humans. But the destiny of humanity was now deemed to be in its own hands, not in the hands of the heavenly hosts.

When Confucius took center stage in this drama some six hundred years later, he concluded that it was pointless to speculate about the nature or function of spiritual beings. "Respect ghosts and gods," he said, "but keep a distance." This and hundreds of other revered sayings of Confucius were recorded by the Master's disciples (and, in turn, by their disciples) over a period of some seventy-five years after his death. They were published in various volumes, the most notable of which is known in English as the *Analects*.

It is significant that the *Analects* is written mainly in the form of dialogues, thus pulling the reader into the issues posed. Confucius felt that deep insight requires the thoughts of many people, not just his own. Moreover, because the *Analects* contains so many aphorisms—not organized in a topical manner, and written down not by the Master himself but by his pupils and his pupils' pupils—different readers can select different points for emphasis. Yet I doubt it would be misleading to cite the following aphorism as central to the thoughts of Confucius: "It is man who can make the Way great, and not the Way that can make man great" (cited by Chan, p. 44).

Confucius advocated a society in which rulers lead by moral example rather than by force. It would be a society in which their example carries over into the everyday family and community lives of the common people. In fact, Confucius saw no inherent reason why common people should not receive the same type of training previously reserved for the nobility.

One hundred and fifty years after the death of Confucius, another giant of the tradition, Mencius, observed that the Master had not been entirely clear as to the fundamental nature of human beings. Was man inherently "good," needing only an appropriate education to perfect him, or was he inherently base, needing far more than education? What we now refer to as the *Book of Mencius* vigorously argued the first position.

In the middle of the twelfth century C.E., a great scholar, Chu Hsi, combined the *Analects*, the *Book of Mencius*, and two other works into what might be called the Confucianist canon. The other works were the *Great Learning*, a short blueprint for political and social life, and the *Doctrine of the Mean*, a discourse on human psychology with a somewhat mystical flavor. Jointly known as *The Four Books*, this compilation tried to demonstrate the total harmony of nature, human nature, and the unseen universe—a harmony that is, at its essence, moral.

Confucian Ethics

People raised in the *Four Books* tradition understand that they must use their moral sense in socially beneficial ways. Why *must* they? The *Four Books* do not assert a moral imperative coming directly from God, as in the Abrahamic traditions. Nor do they put faith in morally influenced reincarnation, as in Hindu and Buddhist traditions. From where, then, does the Confucian moral imperative come?

In one sense, Confucianism does not need a metaphysical moral imperative. For its dominant view of human nature, at least since Mencius, has been that people are inherently good. They mainly need education to cultivate their good nature rather than divine commands or fear of retribution in a reincarnated life.

Yet, even setting aside the question of whether people are inherently good, I think that Confucianists actually do have a metaphysical approach to morality. It relates to their reverence for ancestors—a reverence that seems rather similar to the way others revere God (or gods). In fact, ancestors are revered not only for their own sake but because they are deemed to have the ability to intercede with "heavenly powers" on behalf of their progeny. Significantly, the thing ancestors demand of their progeny above all else is to bring no shame to the family.

Given the existence of a moral imperative that stresses the avoidance of shame, Confucian ethics is best described as "virtue ethics." Virtuous rulers are assumed to beget virtuous subjects. Virtuous parents are assumed to beget virtuous children. Virtuous communities set an example for other communities. Virtue is the glue that holds together families, communities, nations, and the world. Virtue is the root of the tree of society; all else are the branches of the tree.

According to Li-Fiu Chen's analysis of the *Four Books*, the core Confucian virtues are filial piety, sincerity, benevolence, loyalty, and reciprocity. But in an important sense, the virtue of reciprocity encompasses all of the virtues. Reciprocity can be seen as the Confucian expression of the golden rule that all cultures espouse in one form or another. In Confucian tradition, reciprocity covers five spheres of human relationships.

Father and son

One might expect that reciprocity in the Confucian father–son relationship refers to mutual *responsibility*. But, surprisingly, it emphasizes mutual *affection*. It recognizes that affection is more common between mother and son than between father and son. One reason is that the father's role as the son's teacher, in Confucian societies, necessarily involves correction of the son's errors, and this can give rise to hard feelings. Therefore, Confucius said, it is important for families to find ways of maintaining bonds of affection between father and son. So, in many traditional Chinese families, fathers have exchanged their sons with other fathers for instructional purposes. (Regrettably, the education of daughters has not been a high priority in any of the religious traditions I have studied.)

Ruler and subject

Mencius said that if a prince treats his ministers as if they were his hands and feet, they will treat him as their belly and heart, as part of their life force. If he treats them as his horses and hounds, very important but not absolutely vital to life, they will treat him as a fellow countryman, with loyalty and honor. But if he treats them as mud and weeds, they will treat him as an enemy. Here, Mencius speaks of mutual *responsibility*, not mutual *affection*. He understands that the vast asymmetry of power between rulers and subjects makes affection less relevant than responsibility.

Husband and wife

Given the patriarchal traditions so common in world history, it is not surprising that the reciprocity Confucius called for between spouses focuses on division of labor rather than on bonds of conjugal love. In addition to patriarchy, however, there is another reason why Confucian thought de-emphasizes romantic love. It fears that such love can so concentrate a couple's attention on themselves and their own children that it might supersede concern for the larger community. This would not be conducive to the social cohesion that Confucius valued so highly.

Old and young

Confucian societies are also rather distinctive in establishing age as a criterion of social status. There is an underlying assumption that age, experience, and wisdom are coincident. Therefore, age should command respect, because wisdom commands respect. Confucius cautioned, however, that it is indeed wisdom, not merely years of seniority, that earns respect. In another masterful insight into the human condition, he said that merely to live on, simply getting older and older, is to be "a useless pest."

Friend and friend

The reciprocity in the first four types of social relationship has a notable element of hierarchy. Father is higher than son; ruler higher than ruled; husband higher than wife; and older higher than younger. But in the relationship between friends, Confucius insisted on a nonhierarchical reciprocity. Otherwise, the friendship would not be true to itself. Friends should act as each other's teacher and critic without any sense of one being superior to the other.

From these examples, it can be seen that the Confucian ideal of reciprocity plays out in a variety of ways. It means different things in different types of relationships. Reciprocity refers mainly to duties, less so to rights. But the basis for the duties ranges from affection, at one end of the spectrum, to power, at the other end. Despite the varieties of reciprocating interaction, however, the ultimate goals are the same. In Confucian ethics, the goals of human relationships are, simultaneously, the individual's personal self-development and the stability of the larger social setting.

Reciprocity and Economic Life

In theory, at least, the Confucian tradition creates a context for modern economic life that can accept the market system of the Western world, but in a way that Tu Wei-ming calls "less individualistic, less self-interested, less adversarial, and less legalistic." It places a high degree of confidence in the ability of civil servants to give wise guidance to business and consumers. This view reflects that of Confucius himself, who seems to have had little interest in the detailed processes of trade. He viewed economic activity as, essentially, an extension of the family and the state.

Confucius saw pursuit of *The Way* as vastly superior to legislatures, formal legal codes, and judiciaries as a means of achieving a harmonious society. Guided by virtuous rulers, the ordinary person, he thought, would also act virtuously. And this, he felt, would at least minimize, and hopefully eliminate, conflicts of interest. If, even then, disputes should arise, arbitration would be a better method of resolution than litigation, in his opinion.

Confucius was realist enough to recognize that most people desire "wealth and rank." While he made no explicit argument for private property, neither did he criticize it. As long as personal wealth was not attained through immoral means, he accepted it as a functionally useful fact of life. He acknowledged that farmers, artisans, and merchants were three vocations, in addition to scholars and government officials, that all societies need in order to function.

Within this framework, vast numbers of intelligent, energetic people raised in the Confucian tradition have devoted themselves to commerce, even while others of equal intelligence and energy have chosen the more prestigious role of government service for their life's work. Confucian values have been reflected in the day-to-day conduct of East Asian commercial life in a number of ways that I will discuss in part III. Key to them all has been the Confucian value of reciprocity, whether in family, in the workplace, or in the community at large.

PART III

FAITH IN THE MARKETPLACE: HOW SHOULD WE BEHAVE?

I ENDED EACH SECTION of part II by highlighting the theme that seems to me to best connect each religion's overall ethical orientation to the challenges of daily economic activity. In Jewish tradition I highlighted the effort to balance pragmatic considerations of economic efficiency against biblical ideals of interpersonal equity and social justice. The key themes of Christian and Islamic thought that I focused on were a concern for human dignity in the former and a concern for communal solidarity in the latter. Actually, these three themes are not separate but overlapping and interlocked; they are shared by all three traditions. Together, they form an inspiring mosaic of Western divine command ethics.

The religious wisdom traditions of the East have somewhat different themes from those of the West. The importance of humility and patience is a quite striking aspect of the Hindu view of economic life. In Buddhism, the theme that seems to resonate most strongly is compassion; while in Confucian thought, it is reciprocity. Yet these, also, are not so much separate themes as they are overlapping and interlocked. Moreover, the mosaic they form is not sharply distinct from that of the Western traditions.

Indeed, if the mosaics of the West and the East were joined, I doubt that a member of any one of the six faith communities would be uncomfortable looking at it. For the marketplace, the mosaic would portray a coherent religious vision of an ideal economic setting. Economic efficiency would not require a sacrifice of human dignity. Economic actors would exhibit mutual compassion, and individual achievement would not be at the expense of communal solidarity. Steady economic and moral improvement would be pursued with humility and patience.

That is a nice vision, to be sure. But, as we all know, the devil is in the details. As Harvey Cox lamented in a controversial book called *The Secular City*, religious preachers often make broad ethical generalizations that are disconnected from the realities that people confront in their everyday secular lives. Real people live their lives, he reminds us, "in a particular place, doing a certain job, faced with specific issues."

So I turn now from the overall ethical frameworks of the various religious traditions to the specific ways that they have distinguished between acceptable and unacceptable behavior in the marketplace. To do this, I will refer to a broad range of real-world situations that I have encountered, directly or indirectly, during the course of my career, and which I have used in ethics seminars that I have been leading during the past several years. I present the cases in a variety of settings—encounters among individual people in the marketplace, decisions that have to be made in privately owned companies, and challenges confronting publicly held multinational corporations. My purpose in doing this is to emphasize that business ethics is something for everyone to be concerned about.

Following the statement of each case, I present a dialogue that reflects some of the major reactions of my seminar participants to the ethical issues posed by the case. Then I show what the various religions have had to say about the issues, demonstrating how religious thought can be brought to bear in making practical ethical decisions in specific situations. Clearly, religious thinking does not necessarily lead to unambiguous ethical decisions. Usually, there is a downside to any ethical decision, no matter how righteous the motivation of the person making the decision. Nevertheless, I hope to demonstrate that religious perspectives add a valuable dimension to the discussion.

5

The Basic Transaction: Religious Ethics of Selling and Buying

Misrepresentation by Sellers

> Bill went on a trip in his five-year-old car and got caught in a terrible downpour. He ran into a two-foot puddle and had to be towed out. The repair company he took the car to—a very reputable firm—assured him that they could fix the car perfectly, although the job would cost $2,000. They offered him a six-month warranty. Bill paid the price and has been driving the car without any problems for more than six months. But it has 80,000 miles on it, and he decides that he doesn't want to push his luck. So he puts a for-sale ad in the local newspaper.
>
> Jonathan responds to the ad, comes to Bill's home, test-drives the car and likes it. He asks Bill if there's anything he should know about the car that isn't obvious. Bill says: "Nothing important; I hope you enjoy the car as much as I have." Jonathan buys the car. Several months later it stops running and Jonathan's mechanic tells him that the engine has some internal rust that must have been caused by water exposure. Jonathan confronts Bill.

Jonathan: Did you know that the car's engine was rusting?
Bill: No I didn't. It had been running just fine.
Jonathan: Well, was it ever in some kind of flood?
Bill: As a matter of fact it was. But I had it completely repaired.
Jonathan: Why didn't you tell me it had been in a flood when I asked you if there was anything about it I should know?

BILL: Because I didn't think it was relevant. It had been completely repaired. Besides, nothing stopped you from having a mechanic look the car over before we closed the deal.

JONATHAN: Even if I had done that—and I guess I should have—I doubt he would have taken the engine apart to look for signs of rust. I still would have trusted you to give me an honest answer to my question.

BILL: Do you think that if you had bought this car from a used-car dealer they would have told you that it had been in a flood?

JONATHAN: Maybe not. But everyone knows how they play the game, so I wouldn't expect them to tell me. That's why I didn't go to a used-car dealer; I came to someone in my own neighborhood.

> He who conceals evidence is sinful at heart.
>
> *Qur'an 2:283*

A clergyman friend of mine recently gave a talk in which he said that religion is opposed to an ethic of *caveat emptor*—let the buyer be on his guard. My own understanding is somewhat different. I see little evidence in the religious traditions I have studied that classic "horsetrading" is considered to be unethical. Buyers and sellers are expected to bargain shrewdly. Each is presumed to have made reasonable efforts to learn what they can of the other's knowledge and intentions. What is unethical is a deliberate effort by one party to deceive the other. Later in this chapter, I will consider what this might mean about a buyer's ethical obligations to a seller; but here I am concerned with the seller's obligations.

Two juxtaposed Qur'anic verses are particularly instructive. Verse 17:35 requires sellers to give the full measure of what they promise. But the very next verse contains the warning: "Do not follow that of which you have no knowledge."

The Jewish sage Maimonides devoted many pages of opinion to the subject. He made it quite clear that sellers need not point out every possible negative characteristic of their goods to prospective buyers. Indeed, they are entitled to accentuate the positive features of their goods and may use all reasonable means to persuade buyers to purchase them. Except in the case of certain professions, which I'll discuss in the next chapter, a merchant's advice to a buyer is not to be considered the reliable advice of a trusted counselor to the buyer. Thus, *caveat emptor*, let the buyer be on his guard, is advice not to be ignored.

On the other hand, and perhaps this is what my clergyman friend had most on his mind, all religious traditions agree that a seller may not deliberately deceive a buyer about the nature of the merchandise. The Prophet Muhammad, for example, is reported to have said: "In the day of Judgment the honest, truthful Muslim merchant will take rank with the martyrs of the faith." A cynic, of course, might argue that this only goes to show how rare it was, or still is, to find an honest merchant. Such cynicism notwithstanding, the *Qur'an* is studded with verses that forbid dishonesty in economic dealings.

Verses 2:282–283 demand full disclosure in the marketplace, saying: "If it is a deal about some merchandise . . . do not suppress any evidence, for he who conceals evidence is sinful of heart." Classic examples of the impact of this injunction include legal rulings by Islamic judges to the effect that persons who buy sheep that have defects that were concealed by the sellers may return them and keep any profit derived from the sheep's milk.

Similarly, Saint Paul issued warnings about such matters to several of his fledgling congregations.

> Do not defraud one another.
>
> *1 Corinthians 7:5*
>
> Do not lie to one another.
>
> *Philippians 3:9*
>
> Let him that stole steal no more.
>
> *Ephesians 4:28*

Martin Luther insisted that faithful Christian merchants must keep their natural greed under the control of their duties to their fellow men. Even John Calvin, who, unlike Luther, viewed trade as a blessed calling and was an important figure in the evolution of modern capitalism, in no way defended deceitful sales practices. And John Wesley's "gain all you can" rule emphasized that a good Christian may not cheat or lie to gain money.

Did Bill, in our case, misrepresent his car to Jonathan and thus deceive him? As Maimonides describes it, misrepresentation can take two forms. A seller can misrepresent either by what he says or by what he fails to say. On the one hand, misrepresentation occurs if a seller presents his merchandise as having favorable characteristics that he knows it does not have and that the buyer cannot feasibly check out. But misrepresentation also occurs if he withholds negative information that a typical buyer would be likely to consider very important and cannot check out.

Jonathan admits that he should have had a mechanic look over the car before he bought it. But, as he tells Bill, there is a good chance that the mechanic would not have detected the beginnings of engine rust. It seems rather clear that Bill's response to Jonathan's question was a deliberate effort to withhold potentially vital information. He could hardly have forgotten about the flood-related repair expense that he had incurred only six months earlier.

In Catholic tradition, Bill's intent to deceive makes him particularly guilty. Intentions are a key factor in Catholic moral manuals. For example, Henry Davis's treatment of disclosure under purchase and sale agreements considers whether a failure to disclose a product defect voids a transaction. He observes that *in law* the answer depends on how material the nondisclosure is. But *morally*, the answer depends also on whether the nondisclosure was intended to deceive or was merely an oversight.

Bernard Häring, in *The Law of Christ,* also discusses the importance of intent in assessing the morality of commercial activity. He uses as an example an agreement between two parties that reflects their mutual understandings but is not drafted in legally enforceable language. He says that the legal mistake does not of itself annul the mutual moral obligations arising from the contract. Morally, neither party should take advantage of the legal loophole. For instance, he says, it would be morally wrong to challenge a last will and testament that does not comply with legal formalities if the challenger knows that the will really did represent the desires of the deceased.

Similarly, an Islamic arbitrator would almost surely pay great attention to what he deems to have been the intentions of the disputants. Islamic tradition emphasizes the importance of *niyya*, or intent, in most aspects of life.

Hindu scripture and commentary does not contain much in the way of specific advice about everyday interactions between buyers and sellers. One exception is *The Laws of Manu*, a work that deals with the nature of the world and of human social relationships. Having been composed by many different priestly scholars over an extended period of time near the beginning of the Common Era, it is a rather disjointed, often self-contradictory, potpourri of ideas. Yet there is a small portion of the text that helps here. It says:

> [The king] should make entirely void anything pledged or sold by fraud, or [any transaction] in which he detects circumvention.
>
> *Laws of Manu 8:165*

Moreover, according to the *Laws of Manu*, Bill's argument that used-car dealers regularly withhold information is no excuse for his own action. "A verbal agreement does not become binding, even when it is well supported," *Manu* says, "if what is said is outside the bounds of justice" (8:164). The moral import of this statement is endorsed by Buddhist and Confucian, as well as Western, religious traditions.

Most people are understandably, and properly, outraged when major corporations are discovered to have deliberately withheld significant negative information about their products. For example, in the summer of 2000, when Mitsubishi Motors admitted that it had systematically concealed customer complaints for more than twenty years, and when Ford and Firestone were each accusing the other of withholding information about tire failures, the media climbed all over them and the public was furious. But do we, as individual actors in the economic marketplace, hold ourselves to the same standards we set for big companies? How many of us would have told Jonathan about our car being in a flood? How many of us, when we put our houses on the market for sale, think it's perfectly all right to paint over the water stains on our walls or otherwise cover up defects that may elicit suspicion on the part of potential buyers? Why do so many of us fail to apply to ourselves the same kinds of ethical criteria that we apply to the companies whose products we buy?

Truth in Advertising

> A leading producer of canned soups is introducing a new low-fat line called "Heartfelt." The company's advertising department has launched an ad campaign that emphasizes both the great taste of the soups and their health benefits. David, one of the department's recent recruits, is having a conversation about the ads with Annie, a long-service employee.

David: I received a letter today from a customer who says that these ads are deliberately misleading. The writer acknowledges that fatty foods are bad for the heart, but she says that the flavor we brag about comes largely from the soups' high salt content, which may be as unhealthy as fat. Of course, we don't mention salt in the ads. I don't quite know what to say in my reply letter, Annie. Can you give me some guidance?

ANNIE: I would be pretty firm in replying. Our ads don't lie. The soups *are* low-fat and they *are* tasty. Our ingredient labels tell anyone who bothers to look what the sodium content of the soup is. We don't have to advertise it, do we? We're simply putting our best foot forward. That's what advertising is supposed to do, isn't it?

DAVID: But, Annie, the customer doesn't say we're lying. Someone can be purposefully misleading without telling an outright lie, and that's what the customer is saying about our ads. Certainly, an ad should put the seller's best foot forward, but the customer says we're wrong to call our soups "Heartfelt" when one of our key flavor ingredients is bad for the cardiovascular system.

ANNIE: Nevertheless, it's the kind of thing the whole food industry does. We couldn't compete if we publicized the salt content, and we couldn't compete by giving the soups some generic low-fat name.

DAVID: But are those our company's only choices? Couldn't we make the soups tasty with less salt and more herbs? And if that's not possible, couldn't we come up with a catchy name for the soups that doesn't imply "good for the heart."

ANNIE: Maybe, but that's the name the marketing department gave them, and it's our job in the advertising department to help beat the competition.

> Keep your conscience clear so that, when you are maligned, those who abuse you for your good conduct in Christ may be put to shame.
>
> *1 Peter 3:16*

I rather doubt that Annie (whether or not she is a Christian) really has a totally clear conscience as she gives David advice about how to answer a letter maligning their company's advertising. But while the spirit of her arguments may be somewhat suspect, I believe that their substance is valid according to religious ethics.

As I noted in discussing the prior case, religious ethics generally gives sellers a right to assume that buyers will make reasonable efforts to investigate the nature of the products that they may want to purchase. Indeed, that is an important reason why Jewish and Islamic law make a big issue about honest weights and measures. The *Qur'an,* for example, says:

> Woe to those who give short measure, who insist on being given full when they take from others, while when they measure or weigh for them, give less.
> *Qur'an 83:1*

The Prophet, who was himself a merchant in his early life, insisted that neither buyer nor seller should be short-changed—that is, that equal values should be exchanged in commercial transactions. For example, he frowned on exchanges of fresh fruit for dried fruit, because the water loss of the dried fruit was indeterminate. Islamic case law is filled with commentary about proper ways of measuring relative values when damages have to be compensated.

In Jewish tradition, not only must the weights and measures be accurate; they must be easy to see and understand. This is particularly important in the case of essentials such as food, compared with luxury items. Many modern food ingredient labels would probably fail this test. They are often printed in very tiny type that is difficult to read, and not every buyer has the knowledge base to know whether x-grams of this ingredient and y-grams of that are high or low. In the case at hand, however, Annie probably has a right to expect that a buyer who wants to eat heart-healthful foods will look carefully at ingredient labels—even if they are printed in small type. Moreover, a health-conscious buyer should be expected to find out how many grams of salt exceed heart-healthful maximums. Annie is correct in pointing this out to David.

While Annie's argument that "everybody does it" would be religiously unacceptable in cases of serious violations of ethical norms, I doubt that calling the soups "Heartfelt" puts the case into that category. Most religious ethicists, I'm sure, would applaud David's desire for a name that does not emphasize the cardiac benefits of the soup, but they probably would agree that a buyer truly concerned about heart-healthful food is unlikely to be fooled simply by the name.

Additionally, if it really were possible to make a flavorful soup with less salt and more herbs, surely the forces of competition would lead some company to make it that way. The other companies would then either have to follow or risk losing market share.

Some other aspects of advertising, not present in this particular case, do raise religious concerns that are worth noting here. One is advertising that disparages the products of others. Comparative ads appear to have been used with increasing frequency since the Federal Trade Commission condoned their use in 1979. Indeed, a number of lawsuits have resulted from this activity, with Brand X complaining that Brand Y's comparative ad falsely and misleadingly slurs Brand X. From a religious perspective, the issue is not just whether Brand Y's ads are factually true or false. The issue is that slander and gossip are offensive per se in most religious traditions. Hence, advertisers should tell what is good about their product and avoid invidious comparisons with other products unless the information would be truly important for making informed buying decisions. (As an aside, I would note the even stronger applicability of this moral instruction to political campaigning. Disparaging a *person* is a worse religious offense than disparaging a *product*.)

Another religious concern relates to advertising that seeks to create what many clerics refer to as "artificial needs" for clearly nonessential items. Consider, for example, the way a line of extraordinarily high-priced women's shawls was promoted. Advertisements said that the shawls were woven out of *pashmina* fibers. These fibers, it was suggested, are much finer than cashmere since they come from a special part of the Himalayan mountain goats that are the source of cashmere. Yet scientific analyses done by skeptics revealed that the fibers of the shawls were identical to cashmere. Indeed, the very word *pashmina* is simply a variant of the Indian word for cashmere. But how many buyers would know that? Again, the issue in religious ethics is not only the truth or falsity of the advertising claims but the effort to create a desire for such extravagant items.

Sale of Harmful Products

> In the summer of 1997, several tobacco company officials admitted, for the first time, that they agreed with medical and statistical findings that linked cigarette smoking to cancer in some sort of causal relation. These admissions prompted the following exchange at a seminar on business ethics.

Sue: How can these people look at themselves in the mirror? They admit that cigarettes cause cancer but keep on selling them.

JANE: I'm not certain they can't give some valid logical reasons why. First of all, no one has demonstrated the causal physiology—whether cigarettes by themselves cause cancer, or cigarettes in connection with other factors. Second, while I'm not a smoker myself, a lot of my friends are, and they get real enjoyment from smoking. Don't they have a right to act foolishly? Besides, most cigarette smokers don't get cancer.

ED: I'll add another argument to Jane's. It's not at all clear that smoking only a few cigarettes now and then will cause harm. If people took responsibility for their actions and smoked more cautiously, why wouldn't it be okay for the manufacturers to sell the cigarettes?

SUE: It might be, if the tobacco companies did everything possible to discourage heavy smoking. But they don't! If anything, they do the opposite. Moreover, nicotine is addictive, so most smokers can't limit themselves to only a few cigarettes now and then. I think the burden of responsibility falls far more heavily on the tobacco companies.

BOB: I agree. Many products, used carelessly, can cause great harm yet can be ethically produced and sold because most people don't regularly abuse them—automobiles, for example. But cigarettes are quite regularly abused and the producers aid and abet that abuse.

ED: I think that's the key. A producer can sell potentially harmful products if there is good reason to think they'll be used responsibly. But it's not ethical to sell products when it is highly likely that they will be used irresponsibly. My problem is that I'm not at all sure that auto manufacturers act responsibly by engineering cars to move at very high speeds and by featuring power and speed in their advertising.

> You shall not insult the deaf,
> or place a stumbling block before the blind.
>
> *Leviticus 19:14*

In an open, competitive marketplace, businesses can pretty much produce and sell whatever they wish, unimpeded by government controls. Except for clear legislative concerns about health and safety or restraint of trade, or in times of war, governments in countries where democratic capitalism prevails do not overtly interfere with that right. Rather, it is the tens of millions of individual customers that guide production and marketing decisions by voting with their money.

Yet the biblical dictum "you shall not place a stumbling block before the blind" has been cited by both Jewish and Christian ethicists as grounds for holding that a vendor should not offer harmful products for sale, whether or not the products may be sold legally. This is a principle that is often difficult to apply, of course. The harmfulness of alcoholic drinks, for example, depends significantly on the quantities consumed, and countless examples can be cited of products that are safe if properly used but unsafe if carelessly used. Automobiles and pharmaceuticals are products of the latter type that come quickly to mind.

Accordingly, Jewish ethicists have been reluctant to declare that certain items should not be sold because they are *per se* unsafe or unsuitable—unless there are purely religious reasons for doing so, such as pork products. Jewish ethics has tended to qualify the basic principle the way that Bob and Ed did in the case at hand. The idea is that potentially harmful products should not be sold to specific purchasers if they are likely to be abused by those particular purchasers. For example, rabbinic authorities have held that the sale of guns to parties who are likely to use them only in self-defense is permissible, but their sale to persons known by the vendor to be violent is considered improper.

To be sure, this qualification creates problems of its own, for merchants of potentially dangerous products have limited ability to know how their customers will use them. Yet Jewish ethics is quite forceful in urging merchants to think carefully about the potentially harmful effects of their products and to make reasonable efforts to find out how their customers plan to use them. I might also note that, notwithstanding the general reluctance to ban entire categories of products, there has been a growing sentiment among modern rabbis that tobacco should be considered as forbidden a substance as heroin and other addictive narcotics.

Within Protestant tradition, John Calvin took a very strong stand on the issue of harmful products. He was particularly adamant that a good Christian may not sell his neighbor "liquid fire" or "minister to his unchastity." John Wesley said that we are to gain all we can only if we do not hurt our neighbor in the process. The gaining must not be at the expense of body, mind, or moral sin.

Calvin asserted that "in regard to everything that God has bestowed upon us, and by which we can aid our neighbor, we are His stewards, and are bound to give an account of our stewardship." Protestant ethicists ever since have said that, since we are all God's stewards, a business cannot produce and sell *anything* just because it is not illegal to do so and customers are willing to pay for it. The responsibilities of stewardship, they say, should lead businesspeople to refrain from selling products or services that are likely to cause harm, either to individual buyers or to society in general.

Laura Nash, in a wide-ranging study of Evangelical Protestant businessmen, found that none spoke of putting his company out of business for reasons of Christian conscience. But there were many examples of businessmen who had turned down contracts or refused to sell certain products for that reason. One example was Jack Eckerd, founder of one of America's largest chains of drug stores. He refused to carry *Playboy* and *Penthouse* magazines in his stores, and he conducted a public campaign to get other stores either not to carry sexually explicit magazines or at least to set up adult-only sections which children were prevented from entering.

Preachers of the social gospel did not convince Americans, or most other populations of the industrialized world, to radically reshape their political and economic macro-institutions, but they undoubtedly did have an impact on a more micro level. Although they mistakenly thought that capitalism was incapable of self-reform, their protests against the seamier side of the system surely influenced many capitalist-affirming legislators. These legislators—Protestant Christians for the most part—voted for government regulations dealing with food and drug production and marketing, as well as with occupational safety, child labor, and other such issues.

While the force and optimism of the social gospel was ended by the horrors of war and totalitarianism, its spirit has persisted in a good deal of Protestant moral teaching about economic affairs. Protestant concerns about product health and safety are mirrored in numerous pronouncements by Catholic clergy. And in Islamic tradition, as I noted in chapter 3 when discussing Islamic mutual funds, a variety of products are considered not only ritually impure, such as pork, alcohol, and tobacco, but also morally unacceptable, such as gambling and various forms of weaponry.

Among the Eastern religious traditions, there is a strong "do no harm" stream of thought. For example, the *Laws of Manu* in the Hindu tradition say:

> One thing mixed with another should not be sold, nor anything that is spoiled, deficient, far away, or concealed.
>
> *Laws of Manu 8:203*

While this statement is aimed mainly at spoiled or otherwise defective products, it has been interpreted to cover harmful products as well. Moreover, Buddhism has an even stronger do-no-harm tradition. When the Buddha said "do not kill," for example, he was referring to more than the wanton murder of human beings. He extended the commandment to the common Hindu practice in his day of animal sacrifices to the gods. His objection in part reflected his skepticism that the gods respond to such entreaties; but, more importantly, he thought such sacrifices were unpardonably cruel. No living creature, he taught, should be killed intentionally, either to propitiate the gods or to advance personal or national interests. The Buddha was a quintessential pacifist (and probably a vegetarian).

Consistent with this overall ethical attitude, when the Buddha spoke of "right livelihood" as a component of the Noble Eightfold Path, he made it quite clear that right livelihood prohibits harming others. Although his specific references to harmful products were mainly to intoxicants, his emphasis on compassionate behavior indicates a much broader concern. In this context, the words of the Dalai Lama are worth hearing.

> I must admit that I find it a bit difficult to make practical suggestions about the application of spiritual values in the field of commerce. This is because competition has such an important role to play. For this reason, the relationship between empathy and profit is necessarily a fragile one.
> It may be objected that the reality of commerce is such that we cannot realistically expect business to put people before profits. But here we must remember that those who run the world's industries and businesses are human beings too. Even the most hardened would surely admit that it is not right to seek profits regardless of consequences. If it were, dealing in drugs would not be wrong. So again, what is required is that each of us develops our compassionate nature. The more we do so, the more commercial enterprises will come to reflect basic human values.
>
> *Ethics for the New Millennium, pp. 196–97*

Pricing of Essential Products

> In many countries, governmental authorities regulate the prices of pharmaceuticals. Some have proposed similar regulations in the United States. Among the consumers most agitated about high pharmaceutical prices are the elderly. In trying to decide whether to support price control legislation, a representative of a senior citizens' organization is interviewing the chief government affairs officer of a leading pharmaceuticals producer.

Senior Citizen: Your industry has one of the highest returns-on-equity of any industry in this country. What explains that fact?

Company Officer: Drug companies take enormous risks. We pour vast sums of money into research, never knowing if and when we'll discover something valuable. Every major new drug costs $100–$500 million dollars to research, develop, test, and get approved by the Food and Drug Administration. If we were not well compensated for taking those risks, we wouldn't have the financial wherewithal to do it.

Senior Citizen: I don't understand how you can say that your business is risky when the rate of return is high year after year, decade after decade. That seems to me mainly attributable to the monopoly your patents give you. Moreover, your industry's claims about the high cost of developing new drugs have never been adequately documented. I recently read in the papers that a former research director of a leading drug company called those claims "a lot of bull," with all kinds of nonresearch costs being defined as research. Tell me, are you able to quantify, for the public record, the considerations that enter your company's pricing decisions?

Company Officer: I can't give you any formula, but I can tell you what some of the most important considerations are. First, of course, is the need to cover our costs plus a profit margin to compensate for the risks I've discussed. Second, we try to estimate the role that the drug will play compared with other costs of treatment for the illness that the drug addresses—costs such as doctor visits, hospitalization, and the like. If the drug can reduce a lot of other costs, we feel justified in charging more for it because of the value added to the consumer. We also have to consider what the prices are of other drugs that are already being used for the same illness; we need to be competitive with those. And, on that score, we have to make judgments about the amount of time that will elapse before other companies come up with drugs similar to or even better than ours. The shorter the time the more we have to charge in order to recoup our costs.

SENIOR CITIZEN: Why are drug prices lower in so many other countries? Why should they be able to control prices yet we can't do it here?

COMPANY OFFICER: The answer is that they are piggy-backing on U.S. risk taking. Very few major drugs have emanated from countries other than the United States. It may seem unfair for consumers in other countries to get a better deal than consumers here, but if our government did what their governments do then everyone would be worse off. Putting on controls here would be cutting off our society's nose to spite another society's face.

SENIOR CITIZEN: In setting your prices, do you give any consideration to the age and income of the patients who will be the greatest consumers of a given drug? That's what the people I represent are most concerned about. Many of them are spending a large part of their Social Security checks in the drug store. They can't afford it.

COMPANY OFFICER: While I wouldn't equate age with ability to pay, as you seem to, I'm well aware that many people, old and young, cannot afford the cost of pharmaceuticals. But, no, that is not a significant factor in our pricing decisions. I'm in no way downplaying its importance, but we feel that helping poor people, whether for drugs or anything else, is the responsibility of the whole society not of specific people or companies.

SENIOR CITIZEN: Would you be willing to help figure out a method of helping poor people pay for essential pharmaceuticals?

COMPANY OFFICER: Definitely, as long as we had some assurance that it wouldn't be a first step on the road to price controls.

> The rule ought to be, not, "I may sell my wares as dear as I can or will," but, "I may sell my wares as dear as I ought, or as is right and fair."
>
> *Martin Luther, Essay on Trade and Usury*

Although he was opposed to many aspects of church dogma and practice, Martin Luther agreed with the church doctrine of "just prices," which can be traced back to the Greek philosophers. He was particularly critical of collusion to raise the prices of essential goods, likening such practices to robbery; and he urged governmental authorities to crack down on monopolies. A similar condemnation of monopoly is a strong element in Islamic ethics of the marketplace.

It is noteworthy, however, that Luther was rather cynical about governmental control of monopoly pricing. As he said in his essay *Trade and Usury,* "Kings and princes have a finger in it themselves, I hear." Moreover, Luther acknowledged, albeit grudgingly, that unless a merchant can "take as much profit on his wares as will reimburse him for their cost and compensate him for his trouble, his labor, and his risk" few people would go into the business world. "How few merchants there would be, and how trade would decline," he said, "if they were to amend this evil rule [of seeking to maximize profits] and put things on a fair and Christian basis." That conclusion sounds remarkably similar to what the drug company officer was telling the senior citizen in our case.

Clarence Walton, a pioneering student of business ethics, observed in his book *The Moral Manager* that there probably is no area of managerial activity that is harder to describe accurately and assess fairly in terms of morality than the pricing of goods and services. As the drug company officer indicated, pricing decisions reflect a composite analysis of costs, risks, competition, and value added to consumers. Religious ethics accepts this list, whether grudgingly or enthusiastically, but urges that the outcome of the analysis be overlaid with an element of compassion, particularly in the case of essential commodities. For example, Bernard Häring, in his moral manual, says: "The moral theologian will not deny the importance of supply and demand as factors in the price structure." But he goes on to say that charging higher than necessary prices for the essentials of life is morally offensive compared with charging high prices for luxuries.

Jewish history during the hundreds of years when self-governing Jewish communities existed within larger non-Jewish societies provides some interesting insights into religious attitudes about pricing. The leadership of these communities had broad authority to regulate prices, yet they generally chose to leave most pricing to the forces of supply and demand. However, reliance on the marketplace was subject to an important qualification. A community was deemed to have both a right and a duty to take steps to assure that all of its residents had reasonable access to the essential commodities of life.

Based on this right, coupled with the dictum "You shall not rob," a complex set of laws of overcharging (called *ona'ah*) evolved. This included definitions of what items were essential (e.g., only food or also the items needed for food preparation). Whatever the definitions, for those commodities considered essential a rule of thumb evolved limiting selling prices to those that would produce a profit margin of not more than one-sixth. However, community standards could permit higher margins. If overcharging was present, various remedies were provided.

In addition to price control of essentials (actual or threatened), regulations were designed to discourage a proliferation of middlemen that would increase costs and, hence, mark up prices. Middlemen were deemed not entitled to markups unless they added processing value to products; for example, milling a farmer's wheat into flour. And to maximize the supply of essentials, exports were restricted and imports encouraged.

Attention to the supply of essentials had some interesting twists. While prices could be controlled on the upside, so too was there an effort to prevent destructive downward price competition for essentials, lest suppliers be driven out of business. To this end, certain types of producer collusion were permitted, as long as the collusion did not drive prices up unreasonably. This might be viewed as a religious antecedent of our own government programs of farm price supports.

Also of interest is the attitude of Jewish community leaders toward imports. Most communities had a clear bias in favor of hometown producers, often denying nonresidents the right to set up new businesses in competition with local businesses. However, new businesses supplying essential goods and services were encouraged to enter, as were suppliers of nonessentials if they provided clearly superior quality or if the hometown producer appeared to be making monopoly profits.

Most of the regulation of essentials dealt with foods. But during the Middle Ages, at times when housing was in short supply, some Jewish communities tried to protect poor tenants in an interesting way. If a prospective tenant for a flat offered a landlord a higher rent than the current tenant was known to be able to afford, and the landlord accepted the offer and evicted the tenant, the community's rabbi could require the property to stay vacant for a year before the new tenant could occupy it. By this procedure, it was hoped that landlords would voluntarily refrain from evicting poor tenants, thus avoiding a comprehensive bureaucratic system of rent controls.

These types of concerns have been evident in modern times in many religious communities. Coming back to the case at hand, I believe that most religious ethicists favor some form of universal medical insurance coverage that would include pharmaceuticals. On the other hand, they seem to recognize that the coverage cannot feasibly include all treatments irrespective of cost or potential benefit, and they seem to recognize that neither the government nor private companies should have to subsidize people of means in order to protect the poor. Religious ethics could provide a meaningful framework, I think, for further dialogue between the drug company officer and the senior citizens' representative.

Similarly, religious ethics might have provided a better basis for discussion of the recent "energy crisis" in California than the heated rhetoric that the media played up. As the prices of gasoline, electricity, and other sources of energy surged in that state during the spring and summer of 2001, outraged consumers cried "foul," while producers responded with claims that they were merely responding to a shortage of supplies in relation to rising demands for energy.

Commenting on the situation, the economics editor of *Newsweek* magazine wrote (May 14 issue, p. 23):

> I'm not saying that these companies are immoral for making a fortune by taking advantage of California's problems. Breaking the law by creating artificial shortage—which has been alleged, but not remotely proven—would be immoral. Taking advantage of a situation? That's what's known as amoral—having no moral values, either good or bad. It's not nice, but it's perfectly legal, and it's the way market players are expected to act.

That analysis of the situation reveals precisely the mindset I described in chapter 1—that is, that market outcomes are expected simply to reflect the unfettered forces of supply and demand. Government officials can inquire as to whether illegal scarcities have been created. But, if that is not the case, then the market is working the way it is supposed to work. Understandably, most energy consumers in California were unable to view the situation quite so dispassionately. Yet few of either the producers or the consumers of energy had thought to consider whether America's religious heritage might offer any useful perspectives on the pricing problem.

If they did, I believe that each side might have backed off a bit. Consumers might have acknowledged that gas-guzzling SUVs and heated swimming pools are examples of the type of extravagant consumption that their own religious traditions frown on. They, and the politicians who cater to them, might have acknowledged that producers have no moral obligation to keep prices low for such nonessential uses of energy.

On the other hand, there were many people for whom the soaring energy prices were, indeed, disastrous—for example, low-income people who simply could not get to work without driving. For such people, energy is as essential as the pharmaceuticals in the case I have been discussing. Hopefully, producers who were urged to be conscious of religious ethics would think more carefully about charging as much as the traffic will bear. They might try, for example, to develop two-tier pricing systems that would aid low-income people, or if that was not feasible, develop rebate programs aimed at low-income families. Such programs might be similar to the senior citizens' discounts that have become so prevalent in American commerce. But my point is not to prescribe what should be done. Rather, it is to reiterate that religious ethics can provide a framework for discussion that can resonate with both consumers and producers.

Buyers' Responsibilities to Sellers

> John is the manager of the local branch of a major department store chain. He is taking an adult education class at his church. The subject is business ethics, and the pastor has been railing against many of the not-nice things that business people are often guilty of. John is one of the only business executives in the class, and he sees most of the other people nodding their heads in vigorous agreement with the pastor's words. John is fully aware that many of the things the pastor is saying are right, but he thinks that the presentation is totally one-sided. He can't contain himself.

JOHN: I'm sorry to interrupt, Reverend Smith, but you don't seem to recognize that it takes two to tango. All I hear you talking about is how businesspeople cheat consumers, but I don't hear a word about how consumers cheat businesses.

REVEREND SMITH: Give us an example.

JOHN: Well, as you all know, I manage a full-service department store. One of our departments sells color televisions and other consumer electronics products. We provide a lot more service than the electronics discount stores on the strip malls—more advice from salespeople, more comfortable showrooms, places for the kids to play while their parents are shopping, things like that. And because this service costs a lot, we charge more for our things. Now, I ask all of you in this class—be honest—how many of you have never come to my store or another full-service store, spent twenty or thirty minutes asking the salesperson all kinds of questions about different brands and different models, used our restrooms, let your kids play in our play area, decided what you want to buy, and then turned around and gone to the discount store to make your purchase?

MARY: What's wrong with that, John? That's the risk you take when you decide to run a full-service store.

JOHN: What's wrong with it is that you're being just as deceptive as a merchant who makes false claims for his product. You're giving every evidence of being a real potential customer when you know very well you're going to buy wherever the price is lowest, meaning at the discount store. You're taking up my salesperson's time, milking him or her for information without letting on that you're not a real customer.

MARY: Well, I don't see it that way. I have a right to shop around and get the best bargain I can.

JOHN: Sure you don't see it my way. You're only concerned with the ethics of businesspeople, not with the ethics of their customers. Let me give you another example, which, I'm sad to say, applies to my own wife's friends. Do you know how many women spend hours in high-fashion dress departments of stores like mine with no intention of buying? They try things on, ask the sales help questions, decide what they want, and then go to so-called "shopping consultants," who buy direct from the manufacturer at wholesale prices. Is that honest? How can you expect me to be totally above board when I am treated like that?

REVEREND SMITH: I think you've got a point, John. Buyers probably do have an obligation not to mislead sellers, and vice versa. On the other hand, you shouldn't be surprised that your customers want to get the lowest prices they can. Besides, just because you've been wronged at times doesn't mean you need to do tit-for-tat.

> Oral deception is more heinous than monetary fraud because restoration is possible in the latter while no restoration is possible in the former.
> The latter concerns one's money while the former affects his person.
>
> *Maimonides, Mishneh Torah: Sales 14:18*

There are many biblical and other religious stories about tit-for-tat cheating—for example, Jacob's tit-for-tat behavior toward his cheating uncle Laban. Yet I'm sure that any cleric, of whatever faith, would second Reverend Smith's advice to John. Just because John feels that his customers often take advantage of him is not a justification for him to cheat them. However, the issue posed in this case is not so much tit-for-tat as whether John or Mary has the better argument from the perspective of religious ethics.

Jewish tradition is more explicit on the subject of buyer responsibilities than the other religions I've studied, which tend to focus mainly on seller responsibilities; so let's start with the Jewish view. In that view, John clearly is correct to be outraged by customers who use his facilities and take up the time of his salespeople even though they have no intention of buying. Jewish strictures against misrepresentation in commercial transactions apply to buyers as well as to sellers. For example, the sages of the Talmud discussed cases where a buyer who intends to deal with Merchant A goes to Merchant B to quiz him about the nature of his wares and bargain over his prices. Not only would that be taking unfair advantage of Merchant B's time, they said, but his very humanity would be violated. Oral deception is worse than monetary fraud, as Maimonides said, because monetary damages can be restored but damages to a person's psyche cannot be.

The Confucian tradition of reciprocity presents some additional perspectives on the subject. Part of the Master's teaching about reciprocity included the concept of *hsin*, the Chinese expression for living up to one's word. Among other things, *hsin* refers to the nature and intentions of one's speech. For Confucius, *hsin* required speech that is honorable, truthful, and sincere. In particular, it was speech or deed aimed at effecting social harmony. How this expansive meaning of *hsin* might affect any specific commercial transaction depends on the context and particular facts of the case. But speech that falsely suggests to a seller that the speaker is a serious potential buyer is hardly conducive to social harmony.

While Confucian tradition is very heavily focused on reciprocity in human affairs, all other religious traditions also include some version of the golden rule of reciprocity as a basic principle in their ethical outlook. Thus, all religious traditions at least imply a responsibility of buyers to sellers, even if they do not say so explicitly.

Buyers and Sellers in Cyberspace

These thoughts about reciprocity have some interesting implications for the ethics of selling and buying in the evolving world of electronic commerce. To the extent that the parties to commercial transactions have reciprocal obligations to be respectful of each other's time and psychic needs, "e-commerce" may be altering the ethical equation.

Electronic commerce is vastly increasing the opportunities for sellers to deceive buyers, because the sellers are invisible and ubiquitous. But their ethical obligation not to deceive is the same in e-commerce as in face-to-face transactions. The situation is changed, however, for buyers who enter cyberspace rather than having person-to-person encounters with human salespeople in brick-and-mortar marketplaces.

Buyers in the person-to-person salesroom have an ethical obligation not to take up the time and psychic energy of the salesperson if they have no intention of buying. But no comparable injustice would seem to be done to a seller when a buyer surfs multiple websites for product information. In cyberspace, a buyer takes up a few nanoseconds of a machine's, not a person's, time. And these nanoseconds are virtually costless to the seller, in either monetary or psychic terms. Indeed, the seller's very creation of the website represents an open invitation to anyone to come and browse. Harking back to our last case, John could not complain that his website was being abused by insincere buyers the way he could complain about their abuse of his store's facilities.

6

Beyond the Basic Transaction: Professional and Other Special Obligations

Professional Ethics

> Many mutual fund companies have had huge success in marketing funds that invest in Eastern Europe and other "emerging markets." Sally, the Chief Investment Officer of a mutual fund organization, is reluctant to offer such a fund because she doesn't think her research department has the expertise to accurately evaluate securities in these strange markets. Indeed, she doubts that most of the companies that offer such funds have the necessary expertise. But Sally is under great pressure from the sales force to create an emerging-markets fund. Sam, the sales manager, confronts her.

Sam: Sally, please tell me why my people should be denied an opportunity to make good commissions just because you have a different view about this product's suitability than most everyone else. I'm particularly annoyed because you know as well as I do that our clients want this product and are simply going to competitors to get it.

Sally: I'll tell you why, Sam. It's because we're not selling corn flakes. We have a special relationship of trust with our clients. They have every right to expect that when they invest thousands of dollars in our funds, they can be confident that we can manage the funds well.

Sam: But we lay out the risks in the prospectus. Why not let our clients decide if they want to take those risks or not?

SALLY: First of all, you know very well that most people don't read the prospectus. Second, would you really want me to say in it that I doubt we have the necessary expertise?

SAM: The whole investment community doesn't think they're breaking faith with their clients, but you do. That sounds like a pretty holier-than-thou stance to me.

> Do not make your oaths a means of deceiving.
> *Qur'an 16:94*

It is ironic that Sam uses the term "holier-than-thou" in his argument with Sally, because there is, indeed, a strong aspect of holiness involved in this situation. Every religious tradition I have studied warns against making, or even implying, promises that cannot be kept. The *Qur'an*, for example, is studded with verses on the subject, such as the one above as well as "O you who believe, fulfill your obligations" (5:1); and "Those who fulfill their trusts and keep their promises [are among those who] will inherit Paradise" (23:8). Similar statements appear in Catholic moral manuals, the *Laws of Manu*, and the sayings of Confucius.

The Confucian doctrine of *hsin*, to which I referred toward the end of the preceding chapter, is particularly interesting in connection with the case at hand. *Hsin* means not only doing what one has said one will do, but doing it skillfully. It is said that Confucius was pleased when one of his disciples declined to become a government official because he felt he was not yet ready to live up to the promises that an official must make to the people. He knew that he was trustworthy, but he also knew that he did not yet have the necessary intellectual or other resources for the job. This aspect of *hsin* puts a substantial ethical burden on sellers, who too often promise what they are unable to do skillfully. The Confucian story about the responsibilities of a government official has parallel implications for sellers of professional services.

Jewish tradition, in fact, explicitly points out that the responsibilities of people in medical, legal, and other professions are different from the responsibilities of most sellers of goods or services. Jewish ethics has tended to view most dealings between buyers and sellers as arms-length negotiations, subject to a prohibition of deliberate deceit. However, it sees that some commercial activities may have the surface appearance of ordinary buyer/seller relationships yet, underneath the surface, involve responsibilities that transcend arms-length bargaining.

Professionals sell their services to earn a living, just like any other sellers. But what they are selling is different from ordinary goods and services, since the buyers of professional services think of the sellers as *trusted counselors*. Consider, for example, accountants who urge their clients to invest in tax shelters but do not disclose that they (the accountants) will receive sales commissions on such investments. Or insurance agents who recommend whole life insurance without disclosing that commissions on such policies are much higher than on term insurance. Or lawyers who urge clients to name them as co-executors of estates without disclosing that an executor's fees can be very handsome. Or surgeons who urge surgery on their patients without fully disclosing alternative courses of treatment. The clients of these professionals have a right to expect more of them.

In each of these cases, the recommendation may in fact be the best for the clients, but a failure to disclose potential conflicts of interest in these situations would not be considered ethical in the religious view, even if secular law does not require disclosure. Why? Because people do not usually select their accountants, insurance agents, lawyers, investment advisers, or doctors the way they select their grocery stores. They select them as trusted counselors. In such relationships, the vendor should hold to a higher standard than simply not to deceive.

In the case at hand, Sally maintains that even a prospectus disclosure of the risks involved in an emerging-markets mutual fund would be insufficient. She observes that it would be quite absurd to simultaneously offer the fund for sale and admit that the firm does not feel qualified to manage it well. The ethical issue is not, as Sam suggests, that Sally's portfolio managers might be able to do the job as well as most others offering such products. The issue revolves around the fact that Sally, who has a fiduciary type of professional responsibility, does not think she can carry out that responsibility properly.

Sam may be correct that his clients want an emerging-markets fund so badly that they will give their business to another firm if his does not offer it. It is perfectly understandable that he wants to give his own commission sales people the same opportunities to make a living as the sales people of other firms. But the biblical injunction against putting stumbling blocks before the blind is as applicable here as it is to the sale of harmful products. Financially unsophisticated clients are particularly vulnerable. From the perspective of religious ethics, Sally correctly senses her responsibility to them.

Board of Director Responsibilities

> Frances, a professor of management at a leading university, has recently been elected a director of a major pharmaceutical company. One of the company's largest-selling drugs for the control of hypertension has shown experimental successes in alleviating some of the more troublesome effects of female menopause. The company has applied for FDA approval of its use for that purpose. Because of this huge new sales potential, the company's stock has been rising sharply.
>
> Frances is attending her first Board of Directors meeting. Jim, the company's president, tells the board he has just learned that the researcher who discovered the drug's possible new use failed to report a 3-percent incidence of migraine-like headaches in the sample population of menopausal women who have been testing the drug's efficacy. The researcher claims he did not report this fact because a 3-percent incidence of severe headaches would not be unusual for any group of menopausal women, regardless of what medications they used.
>
> The company's research director tells the board she did not know that the information had been withheld and has advised further investigation of the headache incidence. The president says that, pending the results of this further investigation, management has decided not to issue a press release on these happenings. None of the other directors challenge this decision, but Frances is not comfortable with it. However, since this is her first board meeting, she is reluctant to voice her discomfort before the entire board and instead asks for a private meeting with Jim, the president.

Frances: The first thing I'd like to know is whether you're going to fire the researcher who withheld the information.

Jim: That's the research director's call. I shouldn't micromanage the situation.

Frances: How can you be sure that the research director really didn't know about the headache findings?

JIM: I can't be sure; but I've never had any reason to distrust her integrity.

FRANCES: Given the tremendous potential of this new drug use, has there been a company-wide committee looking at its various aspects?

JIM: No. I've been personally involved in this project from the beginning.

FRANCES: But with all due respect, Jim, you're not a doctor or a scientist.

JIM: True. But I have twenty-five years of broad experience in this industry. So I know what questions to ask when a new product is in development.

FRANCES: If you've been so personally involved and have such broad experience, why do you call it micromanaging to demand the researcher's termination?

JIM: Because I get the best out of my people when I limit my role to asking questions but not telling them what to do. As a college professor, you should appreciate that.

FRANCES: Well, college professors do have a lot of latitude—but not if students or other innocent people are at risk of being hurt. And speaking of that, it's not only users of the drug who might get hurt. There has been an awful lot of favorable stock market publicity on this drug. Don't you think we owe it to investors to issue a press release?

JIM: No, I don't, for two reasons that are related to your concerns about harming innocent people. First, the stock would probably drop around 10 percent, and all the people who bought it on the strength of the new drug use would get hurt even though there's every reason to believe—at least so far—that this headache thing will not prove to be significant. Second, and even more important to my mind, I don't want to raise doubts about the integrity of the whole company just because of a single overzealous researcher.

FRANCES: It seems to me that a press release would solidify the company's reputation for integrity rather than raise doubts about it. Anyhow, I would like to have an open board discussion of this whole subject as soon as possible. I don't think that their silence at the last meeting necessarily means that they agree with the way it's being handled.

> Do not keep silent at man's behest
> when God commands us to speak.
>
> *Reverend Martin Niemoller*

This statement in Martin Niemoller's last sermon was a demand that Christians speak out against the Nazis. While the issues that Frances is concerned about are not as drastic, neither are her issues trivial, nor is the silence of her fellow board members unusual. Often during my business career, I have witnessed situations where a board member will not openly challenge a controversial statement by management but instead requests a private meeting to air the board member's different opinion.

Of course, there is a place in business, as in one's personal life, for tactful silence. Frances probably was correct to begin with a private meeting with Jim, but seeing that she cannot change his mind, and considering the broad societal implications of the issues involved, religious ethicists would agree that she is correct to insist on a full board discussion.

Membership on a corporate Board of Directors is one of the most complex jobs in the economic world. A director has multiple, overlapping, and sometimes conflicting responsibilities. A director is "hired" by the shareholders to protect and advance their interests. At the same time, a director should be available to act as a trusted counselor to the company's senior management. From the perspective of religious ethics, however, and increasingly in the wording of the corporate governance statutes of many states, corporate directorship carries with it a moral obligation to bring the interests of the larger society to bear on a company's business decisions. That is the attitude Frances wants to bring to the board she has recently joined.

The history of religious thought about the relationships between business enterprises and the larger communities in which they operate is virtually unanimous on this last point. While private property is generally deemed to be a right of citizenship in the community, property owners and the officers and directors who represent them must recognize that they are trustees not only of their own property but trustees who have fiduciary obligations to God and to the community. In the words of the Bible:

> The land is mine; you are but strangers resident with me.
>
> *Leviticus 25:23*

Bribery

> Joe Smith, an American civil engineer, recently left a domestic architectural firm to become manager of the Hong Kong-based Far Eastern division of an international construction company. One of his direct reports, Greg Chou, is a Taiwanese marketing executive who has had positions in several companies in Southeast Asia. Joe and his team have an opportunity to win a huge contract to build public housing in Malaysia. However, they have been led to believe that to win it they will have to pay a million-dollar "consulting fee" to a retired official of the Malaysian Housing Ministry. He is a close friend of a key person in the current ministry who must give his approval before the contract is signed.
>
> Joe is in a quandary. The contract would be the first big win for his division since he joined the company and he really wants to get it. But he has strong feelings against bribery. In his U.S. business experience, he rarely had to do anything more for prospective customers than take them to hockey games and the like—something he considered to be good social interaction with the customers rather than bribery. But a million-dollar "consulting fee" was something quite different in his mind.
>
> Joe's new company has a rule that says, in essence, "abide by the law of the land in which we do business." Malaysia has rather strict laws against bribery. These laws, Joe knows, are often honored in the breach, but sometimes they are vigorously enforced to set an example. Greg is far more complacent about paying the million dollars and is trying to persuade Joe to relax his scruples.

Joe: I'm not naïve, Greg. I know how a lot of business gets done in this part of the world. But not every job requires this kind of payoff. It's rotten. Moreover, I have to admit that I'm nervous in addition to having ethical qualms. Didn't I read not long ago that some big executives in Malaysia were executed for taking bribes?

Greg: That's true, and we both know that this guy will give half of his fee to the minister. But that's between him and the minister. It's their risk, not ours. We wouldn't be breaking Malaysian law by hiring the consultant.

JOE: But wouldn't we be violating the clear intent of the law, if not its letter? Isn't there a serious moral issue here?

GREG: I'm not at all sure. Please elaborate.

JOE: Well, for one thing, the housing would be costing the Malaysian people an extra million dollars.

GREG: Not if we cut our profit margin by a million dollars.

JOE: And cut corners on the quality of the buildings we put up?

GREG: No! Just cut our profit. Normally, we'd make $25 million on a job of this scope; so we'll make $24 million instead. And we'll be providing jobs for hundreds of workers. That's pretty moral, I'd say.

JOE: What if we don't pay the bribe? I'm sure you agree it's a bribe.

GREG: Yes, it's a bribe. But it's a "legal bribe," if I can use that expression. Moreover, if we don't pay it, one of our competitors will. And, knowing them, they will cut corners on quality to make up the difference.

JOE: But we're an industry leader. Shouldn't we be setting an example for our competitors?

GREG: An example that proves what? I think we're talking about a victimless crime. If we pay the million, we get the job at a decent profit, we employ lots of people, and the Malaysians get good quality housing at a competitive price. It's not as if someone else could do the job better at the price we'd be charging. Yes, the minister and his buddy get a million dollars. But who is it coming from? Whose ox is gored?

JOE: Well, first of all, I'd argue that it's coming from our stockholders. We should be making a $25 million profit on this job, not $24 million. Second, it's coming from the Malaysian government; if $24 million is an acceptable profit, we should lower our bid by $1 million and not pay the bribe. Third, it's coming from the people of Malaysia. We're not using our industry position and reputation to stop a rotten practice.

GREG: True, but who says that we have to be heroes? We're businesspeople, not saints. I assure you, Joe, that if we don't pay the consultant another company will and they'll get the contract.

JOE: I don't see how you can assure me of that. Why don't we just try to be the lowest price and highest quality bidder and take our chances? Even if we lose the contract, the word will get around that we don't submit to extortion.

> You must not distort justice; you must not show partiality; and you must not accept bribes, for a bribe blinds the eyes of the wise and subverts the cause of those who are in the right.
>
> *Deuteronomy 16:19*

Religious ethics does not require ordinary people to be heroes except under the most extraordinary circumstances, like resisting forced conversion. Nor does religious ethics always prohibit bribery. The ransoming of hostages, for example, can be a religiously noble act. But the risk of losing a contract by refusing to pay a bribe hardly can be called a heroic act. And while the ransoming of hostages may be religiously ethical, in many situations it can be ethically unwise because it may simply encourage the further taking of hostages. Surely that shoe fits in the case of commercial bribery; paying it once inevitably leads to further demands for it down the road.

The Judeo-Christian position against bribery begins with the Bible's statement that community leaders, particularly judges, may not violate their positions of trust by taking bribes. Although no criminal penalties are prescribed for such behavior, it clearly was considered highly unethical and the prophets denounced it vehemently (which indicates that it must have been as dismayingly frequent an occurrence in ancient Israel as it is in our day). The Bible's negative view of bribes taken by public officials was extended by the rabbis to bribes taken by anyone in a position of trust, not just public officials.

An almost identical position is taken in Islam.

> Any official who takes anything from the public funds without justification will meet his Lord carrying it on himself on the Day of Judgment.
>
> *Hadith of the Prophet*

While this specific injunction related to public officials, Islamic jurists have extended the prohibition of bribery to many persons in positions of trust.

Whether this negative view of bribery applies to minor functionaries is somewhat less clear. For example, what would be the ethical status of a ten-dollar "tip" to speed up the processing of a temporary driver's license in a foreign country? On the one hand, as clerics often emphasize, petty thefts do not occur in isolation. One begets another and the cumulative total may not be petty at all. Yet, on the other hand, clerics have recognized that the "tips" minor functionaries receive in very poor countries are often the only significant income they can look forward to.

In this latter context, an observation by Father Henry Davis in his moral manual written during the Great Depression is noteworthy. While the theft of trifles can be legal but immoral, Davis says, the theft of something substantial can be illegal but moral. It is always illegal to take something substantial from another person, he says, but it is not a violation of Christian morality if the life of the "thief" or a member of his family is at stake and if the thief has no hope of successfully begging alms. He emphasizes, however, that it is all too easy merely to rationalize a theft on the grounds of dire necessity. As an illustration, he cites a domestic servant who takes an employer's property on the rationalization that the servant's wage, which was freely contracted for, is not a living wage.

Western observers are often struck by the widespread existence of bribery in the Eastern world, both in private commerce and public affairs. But they too quickly jump to the conclusion that bribery is not considered unethical in the Eastern societies. This simply is not true. Not only in Malaysia, which is strongly influenced by Islamic ethics, but in most other Asian nations, which are more influenced by Confucian and Buddhist ethics, bribery is prohibited by law, and severe sanctions are prescribed for offenders. It is common for public officials in that part of the world to resign in disgrace when their bribe taking is exposed. Indeed, a bullet in the head—either self-inflicted or inflicted by court order—often follows. Need I point out that execution is never the penalty for bribery in the West?

The systemic bribery that can be observed in many Asian nations does not indicate that the religions and cultures of those lands have different ethical standards regarding bribery than the standards of the Abrahamic traditions. Rather, as one observer has put it, those societies "simply tolerate greater divergence from a common ethical norm because of low pay in public service, long-standing patterns of corruption, and centuries old customs." As an example of how people in poor countries, whether of the East or the West, generally are more willing to tolerate deviations from ethical norms, he cites a conversation he had with a Mexican cab driver. The cabbie told him that he "doesn't mind if the police steal a bit; but they shouldn't steal so much."

Curiously, both in the Abrahamic and the Eastern religious traditions, the focus is on the bribe-taker not the bribe-giver. An analogous asymmetry would be the greater negative focus on prostitutes than on their clients. Yet, just as prostitutes could not exist without johns, neither could bribe-takers exist without bribe-givers. So, in a curious way, there may be some justification for Greg Chou's argument that it's their problem (that is, the minister's and his accomplice) not ours. But there is no ethical tradition that would support his argument that bribery can be a victimless crime.

Lenders and Borrowers

Alex and Jack are senior officers of a large life insurance company. They are discussing the possible acquisition of a company that specializes in what is known as group creditors' insurance. This is life insurance that consumer loan companies require their borrowers to purchase so that the loans can be repaid in case of the borrower's death.

While the desire of consumer loan companies to protect themselves in this manner is generally acknowledged to be reasonable, the companies have a history of controversial partnering arrangements with group creditors' insurance companies. Borrowers from the consumer loan companies are pressured into buying the policies of the partner insurance companies, which charge high premiums. The partner insurance companies, in turn, pay sales commissions to the loan companies. The borrowers are given little or nothing in the way of information about possible alternatives. Alex and Jack are considering whether the ethics of these arrangements should affect their company's decision about whether to proceed with the acquisition.

Alex: Would you agree that the sales commissions received by the loan companies are a way for them to circumvent the usury laws of their states?

Jack: Not really. Life insurance companies have to pay sales commissions to someone in order to write new business. What's the difference whether they pay commissions to agents of their own companies or to the loan companies?

ALEX: The difference is that sales commissions are supposed to be paid for real effort on the part of salespeople. Here the companies are selling their policies to captive clients. The borrowers have no alternative.

JACK: Sure they have an alternative. The loan companies don't insist that they buy from a particular insurance company, only that they be insured. The borrowers can do some research and buy wherever they can get the best deal.

ALEX: But who does most of the borrowing from consumer loan companies? Certainly not many financially sophisticated people, and they don't really know about the available alternatives.

JACK: But we're not talking about acquiring a loan company, we're talking about acquiring a group creditors' insurance company.

ALEX: Yes, but without any chance of financial success unless it gets business this way. I think we should decline the deal. It's legal, but it doesn't pass the smell test.

> If you lend money to my people, to the poor among you, you shall not deal with them as a creditor; you shall not exact interest from them.
>
> *Exodus 22:25*
>
> If you lend to those from whom you hope to receive, what credit is that to you? . . . lend, expecting nothing in return.
>
> *Luke 6:34-35*
>
> They say that trading is like usury. But trade has been sanctioned and usury forbidden by God.
>
> *Qur'an 2:275*
>
> Excessive interest above the customary rate is not legal.
>
> *Laws of Manu 8:152*

Alex did not refer to any religious smell test, but there is probably no topic in the history of the religious ethics of business that has received more attention than usury and other issues dealing with borrower–lender relationships. Although lenders are not considered to be trusted counselors like doctors or lawyers or other such professionals, most religious traditions have viewed lending as a unique category of business activity. It is a category in which the seller of a service—in this case the lender—must exhibit a special sensitivity to the human dignity of the buyer of the service—the borrower.

The Hebrew Bible clearly prohibited Israelites from charging each other interest on loans, although they could charge and pay interest to foreigners. The negative view of lending at interest was carried forward in the New Testament, where Luke's language can be interpreted as applying to anyone with a good conscience. Subsequent church rulings, however, put non-Christians into an exempted category, which explains why Jews were among the most important financiers of Christian monarchs.

Islamic tradition has denounced the charging of interest even more strongly than the Judeo-Christian tradition. While Jews and Christians ultimately came to think of usury as "excessive" rates of interest, which the *Laws of Manu* suggest was also the attitude of Eastern religions, Islam has to this day continued to define usury as any fixed rate of interest.

The strongly negative religious attitude toward interest probably had two sources. First, in ancient times most loans were to assist farmers or other individuals and families through times of economic difficulty. The loans were thus a form of charity—indeed they were the highest form of charity, since they enabled people to continue to earn a living rather than taking a handout. In such a context, the idea of charging interest on loans was abhorrent.

Second, the concept of capital as a productive factor in the economic process was not widely recognized until the seventeenth and eighteenth centuries, when industrialization and the need for large sums of money to build factories began to make a significant impact on communal life. Prior to that time, only land and labor were apparent sources of economic value. Money seemed valuable only to the extent that its owner himself had a use for it. If not, it seemed only fair that he should lend it to someone who needed it—but without interest, for money was not seen as having what we moderns call a "time value."

The full flavor of the negative view of lending at interest is difficult for moderns to appreciate. For example, the medieval rabbis declared that not only was stipulating and receiving interest prohibited, but also agreeing to pay it. The prohibition was so stringent that all accessories to an illicit loan agreement, including the witnesses, scribe, and guarantor, were considered to have transgressed.

Moreover, disguising interest as a "gift" from the borrower to the lender could not be used to circumvent the prohibition. For example, a borrower could not agree to provide stipulated services to a lender (e.g., to paint his house), nor even to extend a noncustomary public display of homage to the lender. There is little doubt that if the rabbis (or church authorities or Islamic or Hindu jurists, for that matter) had been presented with the facts of the case at hand, they would have agreed with Alex. The insurance sales commissions would be seen as a disguised form of interest designed to circumvent the usury laws and, hence, obnoxious even if not illegal according to civil law.

Of course, these strict attitudes toward lending at interest became increasingly untenable as advanced forms of commercial activity entered the life of religious communities. Even Martin Luther, as passionate as he was about interpreting the Bible literally and as disturbed as he was about the steady encroachment of commercial activity on society, seemed to recognize that an overly strict enforcement of biblical notions probably was impractical. Subsequently, John Calvin argued that the prohibitions referred to noncustomary excessive rates of interest, a view that became widely adopted in the Western world and which had long been adopted in the East.

In addition to Calvin's revisions, there was another way in which the realities of modern commerce were reconciled with religious traditions. It was to redefine not only the term *usury* but also the term *interest* itself. The new idea was that if a loan carried a "profit-sharing" element—a rate of return to the lender that was, in some way, tied to the borrower's profitability—it was not really a loan but was an "investment," and the investor's return was not "interest." While this modification might seem to involve some of the very loopholes that earlier had been condemned, necessity carried the day.

In Islam, there has been a dual approach to the financial challenge of modernity. One is the *mudaraba* company. It is a legal form of doing business that resembles a corporation in which some participants provide the capital while others participate through their labor, experience, and business contacts. If the organization is not profitable, the capital contributors' liability is limited to the amounts contributed. If the *mudaraba* enterprise is profitable, no class of capital contributors may be guaranteed a fixed rate of return. Rather, they share in the profits based on ratios established in the original agreement. It is believed that when Muhammad went to work in his first wife's trading business, this was the type of financial arrangement the business had with its capital suppliers. However, since the *mudaraba* arrangement is only feasible for relatively small and local enterprises, larger and more internationally oriented firms in the Islamic world are permitted to borrow from non-Islamic banks that are not restricted by religious laws against usury.

Aside from the issue of interest rates, what about the principal amounts of loans to borrowers who get into financial difficulty? Here, I think, the humane aspects of religious ethics truly shine.

> If a man is unable to pay a debt and wishes to make a new contract, he may pay the interest that is due and turn around the legal instrument.
>
> *Laws of Manu 8:154*
>
> If a debtor is in want, give him time until his circumstances improve; but if you forgo the debt as charity, that will be to your good, if you really understand.
>
> *Qur'an 2:280*

Clearly, if creditors were told that they could not legally expect to get their money back from distressed debtors, most would be disinclined to lend to the poor, either with or without interest. This situation surely would not be helpful to poor people or to the community. So religious ethics does not deny the legal right of creditors to pursue their rights in courts of law. On the other hand, religious ethics asserts that just because a creditor has the legal right to demand payment, he is not bound to exercise that right. Ethically, he would be expected to delay or even suspend the exercise of his right if the debtor continued to be in precarious economic circumstances.

Yet this expectation can create what economists call "moral hazard." If borrowers expect to be relieved of their debts when they have financial difficulties, they are likely to borrow inordinately. Therefore, religious ethics usually insists that a debtor should be prepared to pay if he is at all able to do so, even if it is somewhat of a hardship.

It is noteworthy that the ancient ethic of making non–interest-bearing loans to persons in need persists to the present time in a variety of religious institutions. In Judaism, the tradition I am most familiar with, they are known as "free loan societies." In such arrangements, people of means contribute to a pool of money which is used to make interest-free loans to needy individuals. The borrowers typically use the funds to pay tuition for skills-improvement courses, or to buy a used car so they can get to a job outside of public transportation range, or even to open a small business. In other words, the loans are used to help needy persons become self-sufficient. The loans are expected to be repaid (without interest), either by the borrowers or by their friends or family, who guarantee the loans. The repayments replenish the pool of funds so new loans can be made.

While all of this may seem a far cry from the kind of arrangement Alex and Jack were debating, I'm not at all sure it is. I vote with Alex. Decline the deal!

7

Ethics in the Workplace

The "New Employment Contract"

For most of its thirty-year history, Anchor Company has been a computer outsourcer serving financial institutions. But in the past six years, management has pursued a market diversification strategy. Through start-ups and acquisitions, Anchor has been trying to develop a manufacturing clientele in addition to its financial services market. However, the strategy has not worked. Management has decided to stop throwing good money after bad and to concentrate once again on its core financial market. This decision means that about 10 percent of Anchor's workforce have to be terminated.

Anchor's chairman and president, who were the prime movers of the diversification strategy, have been advised by their lawyers that an across-the-board cutback would be the procedure least likely to incur sustainable lawsuits. Employees of all ages would be affected in equal proportions. The start-up and acquired operations would fare no worse or better than the core operations. It would be apparent to all that no favoritism had been shown to anyone.

Abigail, the chairman, is an Anchor veteran who became head of the company seven years ago. The ethical aspects of the legal advice trouble her, because she and her predecessors had always stressed the importance of mutual loyalty between the company and its employees. Thus, she would like to give employment preference to the longest-service people. Linda, the president of the company, is considerably younger than Abigail. A woman whose career was molded in the rugged business and physical environment of the Rocky Mountains, Linda is also troubled, but for a different reason. She believes that performance, not loyalty, is what matters most. Thus, she would like to give preference to the most productive people. She is discussing the issue with Abigail.

LINDA: You know that I want to keep the best workers and lay off the least competent, and it doesn't take a genius to figure out which ones these are. But I must admit that I don't know any way to prove it objectively, to either a judge or a jury. So I think we should take the lawyers' advice and cut across the board.

ABIGAIL: Linda, that would cut people who've given most of their lives to this company or to the companies we acquired. Not only have they been loyal, but many of them could not get good new jobs. They're too old for that yet too young to retire and stay home. While you may not be able to prove objectively who the most and least competent workers are, there's no question about which ones have the most seniority.

LINDA: But the most senior workers are usually the most tired out and the least productive. We'd be stacking the deck against ourselves. The business environment has changed. People no longer expect to work at the same place forever. The *new employment contract*, if I can use that term, only obliges a company to give its workforce the most skills it can, not to assure them they'll have a job as long as the company stays in business.

ABIGAIL: Why are you equating age with productivity? I'm not exactly a spring chicken, but I'd hardly consider myself tired and unproductive. As for the term *new employment contract*, I know a lot of people talk about it but I have several objections to it. First, it seems to me more a unilateral declaration of terms by management than a contract resulting from a two-way negotiation. Second, while newer workers may understand the deal you're describing, most of the others signed up for a very different deal. When they came to work, they were told that long, loyal service would be rewarded by company loyalty to them. Third, I don't really think the term *contract* is very helpful except in a labor union situation. We're not a union company that puts a lot of emphasis on legal rights and responsibilities. This company's tradition thinks of the workplace more as a family than a contractual relationship with the employees.

LINDA: Okay, but even families don't stay the same forever. Divorces are very common these days. Married people don't expect the same things from each other that they used to.

ABIGAIL: Is that something to be pleased with? And another thing that bothers me is that the whole burden of this cutback seems to be falling on people who had nothing to do with our decision to expand the business. How about you and me, and our whole management team, taking a voluntary cut of 10 percent in our compensation as we lay off 10 percent of our workforce because we made a bad business decision?

LINDA: I'd go along with that, but I doubt you'd get many of the others to agree. In fact, we'd risk losing many of them to our competitors if we even suggested it. It's hard enough to keep them as it is, with the value of their stock options falling because our diversification isn't working.

ABIGAIL: Okay, so let's just the two of us take the cut and announce it publicly. It will be a signal that we're all in this together. It will sure be a very different signal from the one sent by companies that give huge severance packages to CEOs they terminate in the wake of mounting losses.

> You shall enjoy the fruit of your labors.
>
> *Psalm 128:2*

In the Judeo-Christian view, as well as in all of the religious traditions I have studied, employment confers dignity on people. It is a rather different view from that of the classical Greek and Roman philosophers who disdained "menial" labor. Notwithstanding this basic agreement among the various religions about the dignity of work, however, there are some differences in their understandings about the nature of the *workplace*. These differences need to be explored in order to come to grips with the ethical issues raised by this case.

Jewish thought, as I understand it, has tended to view the employer–employee relationship as essentially "contractual." The obligations of the parties are encompassed by concrete understandings that they have mutually agreed to—or which are assumed by community custom or reflected in community legislation. Subject to some important qualifications that I will describe, this approach to the workplace is similar to Jewish views about buyer–seller relationships. As I showed in chapter 5, Jewish tradition has tended to think of buyers and sellers as arms-length bargainers—except for people in positions of special trust.

Christians and Confucians, on the other hand, have tended to see the workplace in what can be called a "covenantal" context. This approach has contractual aspects but goes far beyond contract. It sees the employment relationship as somewhat like that of a marriage and family. There are, of course, concrete obligations within a family (as there are in the biblical covenant between God and the people of Israel). But family members are supposed to have a sense of communal caring that entails much broader mutual responsibilities (as the Bible describes the extracontractual relationship between God and Israel).

Thus, a *covenantal* relationship differs from a *contractual* one in a significant way. Whereas a covenant focuses mainly on the mutual relationship of the parties, a contract focuses mainly on the rights and responsibilities of each party, not necessarily to each other (although that may be a part of the agreement). In a contractual relationship, neither party should be surprised when the other interprets the terms of the agreement self-interestedly. This is a rather different perspective from that implied by a covenantal relationship.

In the case at hand, Abigail clearly seems to think of her managerial responsibilities in a covenantal sense, whereas Linda has much more of a contractual attitude. Both agree that layoffs are necessary, but Abigail focuses on bonds of mutual loyalty whereas Linda focuses on worker productivity and legal issues. Yet even looking at it in a contractual way, when Linda speaks of a "new employment contract," Abigail seems right to object that the veteran workers—and maybe even the newer ones—never were asked to sign on to a new relationship. They knew they were working for a firm that has always treated its employees like members of an extended family.

While Anchor's business activities are concentrated mainly in the United States, the ethical issues raised in this case are present in many multinational corporations as well. So, in thinking about the contractual and the covenantal views of the workplace, we really need to know more about their implications for a global marketplace. And, in that context, we also need to take a look at how Muslims, Hindus, and Buddhists have thought about the workplace.

The Contractual Perspective

Isaac Herzog, a former Chief Rabbi of the State of Israel, has written about the contractual view of the workplace. He opines that when workers can find employment elsewhere without much trouble, or when employers can fairly easily find other workers at the same pay, they have no ethical obligations to each other beyond their agreements. They don't have a right to entertain extracontractual grievances against each other.

Herzog does recognize, however, that it is often easier for employers to find other workers than it is for employees to find other jobs. This power imbalance may mean that some employment agreements reflect subtle elements of coercion. Therefore, while the agreements are usually legally controlling, Herzog urges employers to interpret them with generosity. This is particularly important when the employees are not represented by labor unions.

Jewish attitudes toward workplace ethics do not rely on employer generosity. The tradition has strongly supported employee rights to organize and has strongly endorsed collective bargaining procedures that minimize opportunities for the exercise of coercive power. The prominent role of Jews in the European and American labor movements of the past century has substantial historical precedent. As far back as the days of the Talmud, and perhaps even in Temple days, artisans formed associations for such purposes as training apprentices and establishing times when they would or would not work. Rabbinic rulings in cases regarding these associations served, in subsequent years, as a basis for rulings regarding broader issues of worker organization and collective bargaining.

It is significant, moreover, that while Jewish tradition favors the idea of competent adults freely entering into voluntary employment agreements, the rabbis have insisted that basic ethical values cannot be bargained away by either party. For example, proper employment agreements should not permit employers to so delay the payment of wages that the employees would not be able to support their families. And they should make some provision for sickness and accident pay. In parallel fashion, the rabbis have stressed that employees must give a fair day's work for a fair day's pay. This means, among other things, that they should not take second jobs if it would make them too tired to work properly for their primary employer.

Jewish law and tradition support the right of employees to strike; however, the rabbis have generally considered binding arbitration to be a better method of resolving disputes. Furthermore, strikes antithetical to the overall welfare of the community—for example, by creating artificial shortages of important goods or services—have been seen as coercive on the part of workers. Accordingly, they were restricted at various times by rabbinic courts.

Lest I be misunderstood, I would point out that Jewish ethics of the workplace developed under circumstances where Jews worked mainly for other Jews. Thus, the contractual employment relationship tended to exist *within a Jewish covenantal community*. Within that community, it was considered a high value to go beyond the letter of the law in the interests of solidarity. Hence, I would not want to exaggerate the difference between the Jewish contractual view and the covenantal view, to which I turn next.

The Covenantal Perspective

> Look not only to your own things but also to the things of others.
>
> *Philippians 2:4*
>
> Follow after things which make for peace and which edify one another.
>
> *Romans 14:19*
>
> Servants, be obedient to your masters . . . and, masters, do reciprocally.
>
> *Ephesians 6:5, 9; Colossians 3:22; 4:1*

The letters of Saint Paul are a good place to start looking for the Christian approach to the workplace. Paul championed individual effort and initiative but saw it as truly meaningful only within the context of a mutually supportive community. His call for reciprocity in the master–servant relationship has counterparts, I believe, in the Gospels. As one example, consider the parable of the Laborers in the Vineyard (Matthew 20:1–16). In this story, an employer hires some day laborers at the going rate. He later hires others to work less than a day, without stipulating the wage but indicating that he will pay what is fair. At the end of the day, he pays all of the laborers the full day's rate, including those who worked less than a day. When the full-day workers complain, he points out that they got paid exactly as they had expected and should not be envious of others who got more than expected. He concludes with an enigmatic statement that the first shall be last and the last first.

On a high theological level, this story may been seen as a parable about

God's merciful nature. God does not dispense grace in a carefully calculated, quid-pro-quo fashion. At a broad societal level, it might be seen to be a defense of economic equality. At the level of the religious politics of Matthew's time, the full-day workers, who were hired first, might represent traditional Jews, and the part-day workers, who were hired last, might represent followers of Jesus.

But I think the parable can also be read in the context of daily workplace ethics. It suggests to me that there are some types of people with whom a stipulated agreement is necessary, whereas there are others with whom a handshake of good faith is sufficient. In this context, I think the parable teaches that those who deal in good faith are to be preferred. The last workers, who trusted that they would be paid fairly, received the same compensation as the earlier workers, who had a stipulated agreement. Of course, there would also be a reciprocal responsibility of the employer to behave in such a way as to be deserving of the trust.

These examples from Paul's letters and the Gospels suggest a New Testament view of the workplace as a close-knit community—a family, in Abigail's terms. This view is reflected in both Catholic and Protestant teachings.

Catholic teaching incorporates contractual notions but broadens them substantially. For example, the first major papal encyclical on issues of economic and social justice, *Rerum Novarum*, was subtitled *The Condition of Labor*. In it Pope Leo XIII put the church's voice behind the need for laboring people to have employment agreements that would provide livable wages and sound working conditions. By implication, if not by explicit statement, he supported their right to strike if it became clearly necessary, and he was highly critical of those who used violent methods of stifling collective bargaining.

When Pope John Paul II issued *Centesimus Annus* in 1991, the one-hundredth anniversary of Leo XIII's ground-breaking encyclical, the rights of labor to organize and bargain the contractual terms of work were no longer a matter of controversy, at least not in the industrialized nations of the world. In his encyclical, John Paul II reiterated the church's support of workers' rights but focused not so much on collective bargaining processes as on the basic purpose of a business firm. That purpose, he said, "is to be found in its very existence as a community of persons . . . at the service of the whole of society" (section 17). This statement, I believe, reflects far more of a covenantal than a contractual perspective on the workplace.

The covenantal perspective can be observed also in Catholic moral manuals. In Father Davis's work, to which I have referred several times, a section on employer–employee relations recognizes that there are contractual aspects that must be upheld but observes that labor contracts "beget real duties of conscience both in employer and employee." To illustrate, Davis asserts that wage levels should, if at all possible, be based on the normal needs of a family with several children, even though such a wage level would provide unmarried workers with an even higher standard of living. Reciprocally, workers "should not arouse against their master unfounded discontent."

Bernard Häring's moral manual also claims that the employer–employee relationship entails moral obligations that go beyond their stipulated agreements. He describes them as "partners" who should demonstrate a "true familial spirit of love." It is noteworthy that one of the moral obligations he cites is avoidance of gender discrimination in pay scales.

Support for a covenantal view of the workplace has come not only from Catholic clergymen but also from Protestant clerics, especially those in the social gospel tradition. While the emphasis of Protestant theology on individual responsibility might be expected to have resulted in support for a contractual approach to the workplace, that has not actually been the case. Indeed, it is noteworthy that many highly successful businesspeople who are evangelical Protestants have been widely lauded in Christian circles for their strong covenantal stance.

One of these businesspeople is Max De Pree, leader of a major office furniture company, Herman Miller, Inc., and a prominent lay leader in the evangelical community. In *Leadership Is an Art*, a book on his management practices, De Pree gives numerous examples of how a business can prosper when its employees are made to feel not only that they have rights but that "they belong." Contrary to the feelings of managers like Linda in our case, De Pree believes that a covenantal type of business firm is likely to respond more effectively to competitive pressures than a contractual type. In his opinion, a covenantal relationship, being based on shared commitments to goals and values, permits greater flexibility. Rather than simply downsizing, he says, everyone focuses on thinking up new ways to beat the competitors.

I must emphasize, however, that the individualistic approach that Protestants traditionally have taken to the interpretation of scripture makes it very difficult to characterize "the Protestant view" on ethical issues. While it is true that any religious tradition typically exhibits a spectrum of opinions on any given ethical conundrum, the observation is particularly characteristic of Protestant Christianity. Even within Protestant denominations, much less across denominations, there is a spectrum of views. For example, Daniel McGee, in an essay entitled "Business Ethics among Baptists," has suggested that a pro-labor position tends to dominate Baptists in the northern United States whereas Southern Baptists tend to be more pro-capital. (The essay appears in a very useful anthology, *Spiritual Goods: Faith Traditions and the Practice of Business*, recently issued by the Society for Business Ethics.)

> The masses ought to be cherished,
> Not oppressed
> For it is only the masses who are the root of the state,
> And where this root is firm, the state will be stable.
> From *The Book of Mencius*

As this ancient statement suggests, Confucian tradition leans strongly toward a covenantal view of society. It is a view that translates into workplace attitudes that are even more focused on the firm as a family than the Christian approach I have just described. The Confucian view begins by positing a reciprocal and interdependent relationship between an educated elite who govern society and the uncultured masses they govern. The masses look to the leaders for protection and for their example of virtuous behavior, while the leaders depend on the masses to provide the base from which the society can grow and flourish.

The Confucian model of the proper relationship between the governors and the governed has its counterpart in the model for parent and child relationships. These ethics of both government and family then carry over to ethics in the workplace. Managers are supposed to exhibit a benevolent concern for the welfare of their subordinates, and subordinates are supposed to show a corresponding loyalty, obedience, and trust in relation to their managers.

Chinese businesses, whether on the mainland or in areas where expatriates have settled, have tended to be family-owned, family-run, and managed as extended families, even when extremely large. Japanese businesses have more often been corporations run by professional managers. Yet they, as well as Korean and other East Asian managers brought up with Confucian values, have tended to run their corporations as if they were family enterprises.

It is true, of course, that there are many cases of exploitation of workers by management in Confucian societies, as there are in Western societies. But there probably are fewer examples in Western societies than in Confucian societies of employer–employee relationships involving a strong element of reciprocal trust and loyalty—relationships that I refer to as "covenantal" in contrast to "contractual." Particularly in recent years, the attitude of Western managers, like Abigail in our case, and like Max De Pree, is the exception rather than the rule.

Middle-of-the-Road Perspectives

> The Lord looks favorably on those whose affairs are settled by mutual consultation.
>
> *Qur'an 42:38*

Reflecting the Islamic value of consensus, Muslim business managers are supposed to consult with employees whose lives will be significantly affected by executive decisions. This does not mean that employees are expected to share responsibility for such decisions. It does mean that they should be consulted and listened to attentively.

Islamic ethics of the workplace recognizes that employment has important contractual elements. Understandings must be spelled out regarding the wages and working conditions to be provided by the employer and the quantity and quality of work to be produced by the employee. The *Qur'an* has an interesting verse in which a daughter says to her father: "O father, employ him. Surely the best to employ is one who is strong and honest" (28:26). Yet the Islamic employment agreement is viewed as far more than a simple commercial transaction. It has strong covenantal qualities. As Sayyed Nasr says, it not only relates the two sides to each other but is entered into under "the witness of God," who demands that the two sides act justly toward each other.

One manifestation of the covenantal aspect of the Islamic workplace is the fact that trade unions are not common in the private sector of Muslim countries. Moreover, while some public sector workers are unionized, collective bargaining in the usual sense does not occur very often. Rodney Wilson has observed that in times of recession Muslim workers tend to favor wage cuts for all rather than layoffs for some. This communal view is reinforced by their sense that the employer is also sharing the burden by lowering his profit goals. In sum, the Islamic view of employer–employee relationships falls in the middle of the contractual–covenantal spectrum.

A combination of contractual and covenantal perspectives is present also in Hindu and Buddhist traditions. There are aspects of Hindu tradition that strike a quite contractual note. Consider, for example, the following extract from the *Laws of Manu.*

> If, out of pride, a hired servant who is not in pain does not do his work as agreed, he should be fined eight "berries" and no wages should be paid to him. But if he has been in pain and, when he is sound again, does [the work] as it was agreed in the beginning, he should get all his wages, even after a long time. If, however, he does not get his work done as agreed, his wages should not be paid to him whether he is in pain or sound, even if the work lacks only a little to be complete.
>
> *Laws of Manu 215–17*

On the other hand, the "business *ashram*," conceived by the Hindu businessmen to whom I referred in chapter 4, strikes a far more covenantal note. Buddhism also occupies a middle position in the contractual–covenantal spectrum. For example, there is a story in which a young man asks the Buddha the meaning of instructions he has received from his dying father to worship in six geographic directions—east, south, west, north, down, and up. The Buddha tells the young man that east refers to parents; south to teachers; west to wife and children; north to friends, relatives, and neighbors; down to servants and employees; and up to religious clergy. Thus, the Buddha accords these various social groupings sacred status—including the working class.

In his discourse to the young man, the Buddha speaks of the responsibilities of employers and employees in terms that have joint contractual and covenantal elements. Work, he says, should be assigned by the employer not only with regard to what he needs from the workers but with due regard to each employee's abilities and capacities. Compensation should not only be specified but should be "adequate" and should specifically cover the workers' medical needs. In addition, employers should share their financial success with their employees via periodic bonuses. The corresponding responsibility of an employee is diligent, honest, and obedient effort. In no way is the employee to attempt to cheat his employer.

Is a Covenantal Approach Sustainable?

In 1997–98, a calamitous disruption of the economies of East Asia, which continued for years afterward, raised serious questions about the viability of a covenantal conception of the workplace. The crisis began when the economy of Thailand became financially overextended and, toward the end of the year, collapsed. The Thai disaster snowballed throughout the region, and the Asian economic miracle of the prior decade became the Asian debacle.

Many Western observers hastened to point out that Confucian values, which Asians had been trumpeting for a decade as superior to Western values, contained some radical flaws. Among these flaws, it was alleged, was "cronyism"—an unhealthy and inefficient blending of governmental, banking, and commercial interests. This cronyism, the Westerners noted, included widespread gift giving (bribery) to public officials honored in Confucian tradition for their supposedly dedicated service to the commonweal. While the critics acknowledged that cronyism and bribery were hardly unknown in Western society, they asserted that it was more inherent in the Confucian emphasis on communal solidarity than in the Western (especially American) emphasis on individualism.

Another alleged flaw was that, in its effort to provide an umbrella of security over its employees, Confucian values had made Asian business firms less able than Western (especially American) firms to respond adequately to the increasingly rapid changes of global economic conditions. It was argued that while many aspects of Asia's community ethos might remain, the region's business firms would probably have to begin looking more like American firms. Coming back to our case study, it would be the kind of firm that Linda champions, not the kind of firm that Abigail and her predecessors had fashioned.

While it is still too early to know for sure whether a covenantal workplace ethic can survive in a globally competitive environment, the first straws in the wind suggest that it cannot. The process of change has begun with rounds of layoffs of redundant workers in Asian enterprises. Asian firms no longer suggest to their workers that they will be lifetime employees; and workers, in turn, feel freer than in the past to join competing companies if they can advance their careers.

The forces of economic globalization have introduced new questions about the very nature of the "family" that a covenantal ethic postulates. The globalization of business involves new employment relationships with workers abroad whose interests are often in conflict with the interests of domestic workers. Thus, even if a business manager tried to focus on "the common good," a covenantal view of the workplace is strained by new questions as to which parties have what in common regarding their good.

Yet religious ethics is insistent that people of faith must try to make a difference in the moral conduct of the marketplace. As this demand is applied to the workplace, it requires that human beings not be treated as mere commodities, mere instruments to facilitate the production and distribution of goods and services. What is needed, I think, is a way to fuse the contractual and the covenantal approaches rather than put them into diametric opposition.

The "new employment contract" that Linda espouses may, in fact, be the answer, but only, as Abigail asserts, if it is developed in a mutually determined and mutually understood way rather than simply being imposed by management. Done well, it can develop not only specific terms and conditions of employment but can be used as a vehicle for enlarging the commitments by both parties to each other. Moreover, it does not necessarily require the spread of formal trade unions. It can maintain the individuality so prized in the competitive economic world without sacrificing cooperation among employees and between employers and employees. It need not make jobs secure irrespective of an individual's or the firm's performance; but it would make managers think more carefully about how they go about making drastic changes that affect the lives of the people who report to them.

Ethics of Part-Time Employment

Jones Company is a leading mail-order, and now e-commerce, vendor of casual clothing. It is publicly owned, but the company has long been run by members of the founding family. Ever since Horace Jones started the company, almost sixty years ago, it has fostered a warm, caring environment for its employees. This reflected Horace's faith, which he inculcated in his children, that the "table fellowship" of early Christian days established a model that should pervade all aspects of human relationships, including the workplace.

The Jones Company has thrived and has been repeatedly written up in the press for the way it has blended religious belief with business acumen. In the past five years, however, competitors have been making inroads into Jones's market by offering similar products at lower prices. The competitors have been able to afford this pricing strategy by hiring part-time hourly-wage help for peak periods of the day and peak seasons, whereas all of Jones Company's workers are full-time salaried people with handsome fringe benefits.

Jones tackles the problem of daily and seasonal peaks and troughs with a system of flexible hours and flexible vacation time that the employees helped to design. Nevertheless, it is a more costly way of doing business. The younger members of the company's management team, grandchildren of the founder, are worried that if Jones Company does not start using part-timers on a regular basis it may become a marginal entity in the industry in less than ten years. Horace Jones, Jr., the sixty-two-year-old current CEO of the company, is having an intense discussion of the subject with his daughter, Jane, who is being groomed to become Chief Operating Officer.

JANE: Dad, I could not have grown to adulthood without knowing and appreciating Grandpa's and your philosophy. I wish we could continue with it, but we just can't. The way things are going, not only will I and my cousins have difficulty keeping this company viable, but our workers, who mean so much to all of us, will suffer also, because we're not going to be able to compete. Besides, it's not as if we have to put everyone on part-time, and we don't have to make radical moves all at once. We can move toward part-time over a period of three or four years by replacing full-timers as they retire or leave and by creating an incentive program that encourages early retirements. As we move that way, we can gradually reduce our prices to get closer and closer to our competitors. Our profits will be squeezed a bit, but not severely, and I doubt our stock price will get hurt too much because investors will see that we're moving in the right direction.

HORACE: I know what you're saying, Jane, but I think you and your cousins are missing something important. Maybe our competitors can undercut us for a while. But I believe strongly that, over time, the productivity of their workers will deteriorate compared with our people. You can't tell me that the morale, and therefore the work effort, of a bunch of part-time people can be as high as that of people who are treated as members of the family. Don't you think that mutual loyalty matters?

JANE: Sure it matters, Dad, but not for everybody in the same way. Maybe I'm missing something, but so are you when you talk like this. What makes you so sure that everyone wants to feel like part of the Jones family, or of any other company family? There's a reason why Manpower Inc. and other temporary employment agencies have become gigantic businesses. The reason is that a lot of people don't want to feel married to their company. They want a looser kind of working relationship so they can devote more of their energies to their personal lives, to their table fellowships away from the job. Part-time work is just one aspect of a different kind of lifestyle from the one you and Grandpa cherished. There's no reason why part-timers won't work just as hard as full-timers, as long as we treat them with dignity and respect, pay them competitive wages, and involve them in the design of their work the same way we've done with our full-timers.

HORACE: I don't see our competitors treating them that way. It seems to me that part-timers are treated like replacement parts in a machine, commodities that you buy and throw away at your convenience.

JANE: You're right about that. But maybe we can get a competitive advantage by treating them differently. I'm not challenging your ethics; I think I'm just as good a Christian as you. What I'm challenging is the way you insist that the ethics have to be implemented.

HORACE: Aren't you afraid that our full-timers will see a move toward part-timers as just the first shoe to drop. Won't they start to worry about their own security?

JANE: That depends on whether we handle it well or not, Dad.

> Every economic decision and institution must be judged in light of whether it protects or undermines the dignity of the human person.
>
> *Economic Justice for All, paragraph 13*

This statement emanated from the U.S. Catholic Bishops' Conference in 1986. It not only reflects the views of the Catholic Church but captures the ethics of all religious traditions, especially with regard to the workplace. It is at the core of the debate between Jane and her father.

Horace is concerned that the human dignity of part-time workers cannot be protected and maintained the way the dignity of full-time workers can be. Jane says, "it all depends on whether we handle it well or not." She wants to find new ways to have a flexible labor force without compromising the ethical values that she and her father both hold dear.

Jane believes that Jones Company can be competitive and ethical at the same time. There are two critical factors, she thinks. The first is to make the transition mainly through attrition and early-retirement incentives rather than the massive layoffs with little or no notice that are all too common in many enterprises. Jane's ethics would not countenance the "five o'clock massacres" in which dismissed employees are suddenly told not to return the next day—not even to pick up their personal belongings for fear that they will disrupt the remaining employees. The type of early-retirement incentive program she probably would favor would doubtless include lump-sum payments and pension acceleration, but might also include retraining assistance and relocation loans.

The second critical factor in the transition that Jane envisions is to involve the new part-time workers in the structuring of their jobs. Moreover, since the full-timers are already accustomed to that process, they should be included in the discussions to minimize possible frictions between the remaining full-timers and the new part-timers. What Jane envisions, in effect, is an extension of the "new employment contract" idea to the sphere of part-time work.

Of course, Jane cannot be certain that her approach is really feasible. What she can be more certain of is that her father's and grandfather's "we're all one big family" philosophy is no longer viable. Something has to take its place that will enable Jones Company to be more competitive without violating the company's history of treating its employees justly and respectfully.

Taking Disciplinary Action

> Merit Bank will match up to $10,000 per year of an employee's contributions to IRS-qualified charitable institutions. The plan requires the contributions to be from the employee's personal funds or the funds of his or her spouse.

Marie, a long-service clerk at the bank, has a disabled son who attends an excellent special-needs school that qualifies for matching contributions under the plan. She is active in the parents' association of the school and knows that it is particularly hard-pressed financially this year. Marie and her husband typically make a $2,500 donation, in addition to tuition, which the bank matches. Marie's brother, who does not work at the bank, also donates $2,500 to the school.

Because of the school's financial strain, Marie asks her brother to give his $2,500 to her, so that she can add it to her own donation and have the bank match the full $5,000 rather than only her $2,500. She intends to indemnify him for the tax saving that he will lose by not sending his donation directly to the school.

When the bank's Personnel Department receives Marie's request for a $5,000 match, and compares it with prior years, they become suspicious. They interview Marie and she acknowledges what she has done. Her only excuse, she says, is that the school needs the money desperately and she knows that if she could have afforded $5,000 the bank would have matched it without any question. The personnel officer, Mark, decides to consult with the bank's comptroller, Gene, and the two of them are discussing the case.

GENE: I'm outraged. By deliberately violating this policy, Marie was trying to steal money from the bank. We have zero tolerance for stealing company funds, and I think we have no choice but to terminate her.

MARK: I certainly think she should be severely disciplined, perhaps by suspending any salary increases for a few years, but I don't think we should fire her. She has a long and spotless history of good work for our company. It's not as if she tried to put bank money in her own pocket. The money would have gone to a good cause.

GENE: Stealing from the bank for a good cause doesn't make the theft right. Besides, I'm not sure I agree that she wouldn't benefit personally. After all, her son is receiving services from the school, and Marie gets the prestige that comes with our matching gift in her behalf.

MARK: Tell me, Gene, when we match our CEO's donations to his alma mater and his relatives get favored treatment when they apply for admission, isn't he receiving services? And when he instructs our community affairs people to take ten-thousand-dollar tables at fundraising dinners for his favorite charities, isn't he enhancing his own image as well as the bank's?

GENE: Well, rank does have privileges. That's how the world works.

> You must not be partial in judging: hear out the small and the great alike.
>
> *Deuteronomy 1:17*
>
> What destroyed your predecessors was that when a person of rank among them committed a theft they left him alone, but when a weak one of their number committed a theft they inflicted the prescribed punishment on him.
>
> *Hadith of the Prophet*
>
> Where the rod moves about, black and with red eyes, destroying evil, there the subjects do not get confused, as long as the inflicter sees well.
>
> *Laws of Manu 7:25*
>
> A man is not on the path of righteousness if he settles matters in haste. A wise man calmly considers what is right and wrong, and faces different opinions with truth, non-violence and peace.
>
> *Dhammapada 256–57*
>
> To be able to judge others by what is near to ourselves may be called the method of realizing humanity.
>
> *Analects 6:28*

The religious traditions of both East and West are unanimous in their advice about the ethics of judgment and punishment. They urge careful deliberation and impartiality. Careful deliberation is necessary because all cases are not alike even though they may appear to be on the surface. Impartiality is a necessary condition of a just society.

This advice is as applicable to the workplace as to every other sphere of life. There is nothing surer to destroy employee morale than a double standard of discipline—where management rushes to judge and punish infractions by rank-and-file workers, while exercising extraordinary caution in assessing and punishing the behavior of senior executives.

Yet it happens all too often. A bookkeeper is terminated for altering a withholding tax record in order to protect a friend. However, it is obvious to all that senior executives often "adjust" their profitability calculations in order to protect their own bonuses. Lower-rung people are severely disciplined for submitting inflated expense vouchers; yet senior executives bring friends and family to the corporate box at the football stadium or take the corporate jet when a commercial flight is readily available.

Gene is correct that rank has privileges, but what is the cost of those privileges in employee morale? Gene speaks of zero tolerance for theft of company funds, but he applies that principle to Marie's abuse of the company's matching gift program and not to the CEO's authorization of company donations to his favorite charities. And Gene interprets a zero tolerance principle to mean that Marie should be fired even though she has, heretofore, had a long and impeccable record of service to the bank.

Does Gene really believe in zero tolerance when he seems willing to tolerate what some people do but not others? There is no disputing the fact that Marie knowingly violated the bank's matching gift policy and should be punished. But punishment can range from verbal reprimands to pay cuts, to demotions, to termination. Gene's response seems too hasty, too severe, and hardly impartial.

8

The Face of the Other

Exporting Jobs to Less-Developed Countries

A large manufacturer of plastic houseware, with plants in several different U.S. locations, is under competitive pricing pressure from companies that manufacture similar products in places such as China and Indonesia. There these competitors have access to very low-wage labor, including child labor, and they are minimally constrained by the type of environmental protection regulations that prevail in the United States.

The firm is privately owned by two aging brothers, Al and Rick. Both are deeply religious men, learned in the ethics not only of their faith but of other faiths as well. Despite their similar grounding in religious ethics, however, the brothers have reached quite different conclusions about whether or not to move at least some of their production abroad. A not insignificant factor in their deliberations is that their Chief Operating Officer is a female, Janet Smith. She and the two brothers are in the midst of one of their frequent discussions about the future of the firm.

Al: I know we're under competitive pressure, but it's not as if the survival of our business is at stake. Yes, we'll have less market share if we keep all of our production here, because we won't be fully competitive in price. But I can live with that. I just don't see how, in good conscience, we can lay off workers in America and give their jobs to exploited children in Asia. Moreover, these countries don't give a darn about the environment and we'd be sanctioning that kind of behavior.

Rick: I don't see why you keep talking about exploiting the children, Al. Their families desperately need the wages they can bring home. It was no different in America in the old days, and it surely wasn't any different in biblical times. Until a community reaches a certain level of material well-being, it can't afford to keep the kids in school. That's true as well about environmental protection. It may be something they'd like but can't yet afford to make a high priority.

AL: I hear you, but carrying your argument to its logical extreme, most of America's low-skilled production jobs will eventually get exported. If most American workers with minimal skills lose their jobs, what happens to *their* children?

RICK: That's not a logical extreme; it's a wild exaggeration. The service industries are booming in America and there are plenty of low-skilled jobs. Anyhow, why are Americans more entitled to jobs than Chinese or Indonesians— or anyone else? They're all God's children.

AL: Certainly they are. But all religions, I think, say that you first take care of those closest to you.

JANET: How about considering the possibility of moving abroad but trying to set an example there by paying better than everyone else? I think we could manage to be price competitive if we paid more than the going wages over there but cut our profit margins slightly. In fact, I've done some calculations that show how we could limit the number of hours any child works and set up on-site schools for their after-work hours. As I say, we'd have to take a slight cut in our profit margins, but we could do it without a major impact on earnings per share. In fact, maybe the example we set would put pressure on our competitors to do the same in their foreign operations.

AL: I don't at all mind making less money, so your thought has some appeal if we really had to move the jobs. But I'm still not convinced that we have to or that it would be fair to our current employees.

RICK: Janet, your thought has some personal appeal to me also; but it has a downside. You know that we've been talking for a long time about going public. Al and I don't have many more working years left, and our children aren't interested in coming into the business. The best thing we can do for you and our other key people, as well as for our children, is to give you all a stake in a strong public company. Wouldn't the reduced profit margins hurt our ability to go public?

JANET: That depends on how much we'd have to cut our margins. If it wasn't too large, we could still go public although maybe at a somewhat lower price.

RICK: Well, Al and I could probably give ourselves a smaller percentage ownership than we now have, and this would minimize the impact of the lower price on Janet and the others. Still, I'm not at all sure that if we were a public company we could continue with Janet's plan. I think that public shareholders might well tell us to stop being do-gooders with their money, unless we were pretty sure that our competitors will follow our lead.

JANET: Maybe, but I'm not so sure. In fact, I think it's possible that if we publicized our unilateral efforts to raise living standards overseas we might actually attract some business we don't have now. Surveys show that some customers are even willing to pay premium prices to producers who set high ethical standards.

AL: I think you're dreaming, Janet. What people say in surveys and what they actually do in the real world are very different. And, speaking of the real world, one of the things we haven't talked much about is how Janet would be treated in China or Indonesia. You know, Confucian and Muslim societies don't exactly welcome women as bosses of their factories.

RICK: That's truer, I think, about their attitude toward women of their own community. I believe they recognize that things are different in America, and while they might not want to make our ways their ways, they'd probably accept Janet's authority because we gave it to her. What do you think, Janet?

JANET: I think they'd be more likely to accept me if I didn't rub my authority in their faces. I'd try, as much as possible, to be the behind-the-scenes policy maker, but have men as the factory floor bosses. Obviously, I'd be gnashing my teeth a lot, because I'm pretty upset about how they treat women. But I think we have to be sensitive to their way of life.

> Do unto others as you would have them do unto you.
> Do not do to others that which is hateful to you.
> *The Golden Rule*

All religious ethical systems preach some version of the golden rule, either in its positive construction (do for others) or its negative version (do not do to others). Yet there is probably no economic issue that generates more heated argument about the application of the golden rule than the transfer of jobs. The case at hand involves transfers from American workers to Asian workers, but it has counterparts all over the world. Domestic workers resent the loss of jobs to foreigners. Even within countries, native citizens resent losing jobs to immigrants. Intertwined with the issue of job exports per se are cultural differences regarding child labor, gender attitudes, environmental protection, and the like.

Who Is My Neighbor?

Golden rule ethics involves attitudes toward, and treatment of, one's neighbors. But what do the various religions have to say about *who one's neighbors are* in the context of potential job exports? Are they American workers or Asian workers? Are they the children of American workers or the working children of Asian families? Are they female American managers or Asian men brought up to believe that women shouldn't be bosses of men?

Religious thought reflects the tension embedded in these questions, the tension of "us versus them," of attitudes toward "the other." It is a tension that seems to be a part of the human condition. Al and Rick, both deeply religious men brought up in the same religious tradition (it doesn't matter which religion for purposes of this discussion), can each find support for his position on exporting jobs from America to lower-cost regions of the world. Perhaps that is why Janet's approach is so intriguing. It offers a possible way of bridging the different attitudes. Let's begin our consideration of the case by examining Judeo-Christian attitudes toward "the other."

> You shall not hate in your heart anyone of your kin; you shall reprove your neighbor, or you will incur guilt yourself.
>
> You shall not take vengeance or bear a grudge against any of your people, but you shall love your neighbor as yourself: I am the Lord.
>
> *Leviticus 19:17-18*

This is one of the most quoted passages in the Bible. But who is the text referring to? Who is "your kin," "your neighbor," "your people"? Who is entitled to the loving concern of Bible-believing people? Arguments can be made for particularist interpretations, like Al's "Americans first" position, or for universalist interpretations, like Rick's reference to "all God's children."

A particularist reader would focus on the text's juxtaposition of "neighbor" with "kin" and "your people." This juxtaposition seems to narrow the requirement of neighbor love to one's immediate family and community. On the other hand, a universalist reader would note that at its very beginning the Bible states that all human beings are created in God's image and have a common ancestry. So, if all human beings are siblings, or at least cousins, the terms *your kin* and *your people* would be referring to all of humanity.

The broader interpretation would seem to be supported by the fact that shortly after the statement, "love your neighbor as yourself," the Bible says:

> When an alien resides with you in your land, you shall not oppress the alien.
>
> The alien who resides with you shall be to you as the citizen among you; you shall love the alien as yourself, for you were aliens in the land of Egypt: I am the Lord your God.
>
> *Leviticus 19:33-34*

This theme is repeated in Deuteronomy (10:19). As Moses sums up the Lord's instructions, he tells the Israelites: "You shall also love the stranger, for you were strangers in the land of Egypt." The rabbis of the Talmud counted several dozen reminders in the Torah of a special obligation to aliens and strangers. Moreover, the New Testament shows that to be a central message of Jesus. Love of neighbor, he insisted, must be understood in the context of love of God, who loves all of humanity. Thus, even enemies are deserving of love.

One does not have to be a Christian to echo Jesus' teaching. The modern Jewish philosopher Emmanuel Levinas, for example, is convinced that when the Torah refers to moral obligation to strangers, it means exactly that, obligation to *all* others. The obligation, moreover, is boundless and often can seem overwhelming. As he puts it, a believer's obligation is "to support the universe"; it is "a crushing charge, but a divine discomfort."

Yet it is hard to deny that there is ambivalence in the biblical language, especially when it is put into the cultural context of ancient Israel. The Torah is not consistent in the way it uses its own term for neighbor, *re'a*. In an essay entitled "The Neighbor (Re'a) Whom We Shall Love," Ernst Simon has cited many examples of the ambivalent Torah language, including the following:

> When Moses went out of Pharaoh's palace to his Jewish brothers he found them fighting. Turning to the offender, he said, "Why do you strike your fellow [*re'akha*]?" (Exod. 2:13). In this case it is clear that both contenders are Jews so that the term *re'a* refers here only to another Jew. A bit later we find a case where *re'a* refers specifically to a neighbor who is a non-Jew. God instructs Moses to command the Israelites who are about to leave Egypt "that each man shall ask of his neighbor [*re'ehu*] and each woman of her neighbor [*re'utha*], jewels of silver, and jewels of gold." (Exod. 11:2)

Beyond the ambivalent biblical uses of the word "neighbor," history tells us that ancient Israel distinguished between two classes of "strangers." There were "resident aliens," on the one hand, and "foreigners," on the other. The latter, whose sojourn in the land was considered temporary, were protected mainly by folkway courtesies rather than by the religious law of the land.

The folkway courtesies were reminiscent of Abraham's open-handed welcoming of strangers into his home. But that made foreigners dependent on generosity rather than rights. Foreigners were not entitled to the benefits of interest-free loans, for example (Deuteronomy 23:21), or to calendric periods of loan remissions (Deuteronomy 15:3), whereas resident aliens were. Even resident aliens, moreover, who were considered a much more integral part of the Jewish community and enjoyed rights that were in many ways equal to those of Jews, were socially stratified. For example, the Holiness Code warned Israelites not to enslave their needy kinsmen (Leviticus 25:39) but specifically permitted the children of resident aliens to be slaves (Leviticus 25:45–46).

Nor does one have to look only at discussions about strangers to conclude that the Bible is ambivalent about the meaning of love of neighbor.

The text is filled with evidence that siblings and cousins—even some of the most admired personalities in Judeo-Christian tradition—were hardly models of loving kinsmen. And, surely, the postbiblical history of Christianity does not reveal a broad acceptance of what Jesus taught. The Crusades, the Inquisition, and countless pogroms are only part of the evidence. Beyond those abominations, there is plenty of evidence of "me first" in more prosaic Christian thought.

For example, in the "give all you can" portion of his aphorism: gain all you can; save all you can; and give all you can, John Wesley told his followers to first take care of themselves and their personal households. Then, if a surplus remained, they were to "do good to them that are of the household of faith." Finally, if a surplus still remained, they were to "do good unto all men."

It is important to note, however, that while Wesley said, in effect, "me first," he by no means said "me only," especially when there is a surplus that might be shared with others. That, in a sense, is a central thrust of Rick's position vis-à-vis Al's. It is a position that seems to be echoed in sentiments expressed by the Conference of U.S. Catholic Bishops, such as the following:

> All people have a right to participate in the economic life of society.
>
> All members of society have an obligation to the poor and vulnerable.
>
> *Economic Justice for All (1986), paragraphs 15–16*

Turning from Judeo-Christian to Islamic traditions, we again find ambivalent attitudes about "the other." As best we can tell, Muhammad fully expected that his Jewish neighbors would recognize him as the final link in a long chain of prophets of the One God. Thus, his initial attitude toward them was kindly. But it remained that way only up to the point at which the Jews clearly rejected him. At that point, his kindliness turned to deep resentment. All the more so was Muhammad's resentment of people who not only rejected him but also rejected Allah.

As an example of ambivalent Islamic attitudes toward nonbelievers, consider the following Qur'anic verses. They are juxtaposed closely together in the same sura (the *Qur'an* is divided into sections called *suras*).

> You have an excellent model in Abraham and those who were with him,
> when he said to his people: "We are through with you
> and those you worship other than God; . . .
> I shall ask forgiveness for you, but I have no power to prevail with God for you."
>
> It may be that God will create love between you and your enemies.
>
> God does not forbid you from being kind and acting justly towards those who did not fight over faith with you nor expelled you from your homes.
>
> *Qur'an 60:4, 7, 8*

These verses oscillate between outright rejection of heathens and openness to the possibility of some reconciliation, at least with those who have not been actively hostile. Numerous other verses can be cited, moreover, in which ambivalent attitudes are displayed not only toward heathens but also toward Jews and Christians. The *Qur'an* asserts that Muslims are to respect the Jewish and Christian prophets and their sacred documents, but it does not, on the whole, actively encourage Muslims to treat non-Muslims with loving-kindness. (Might this help explain the participation of Muslim oil-producing countries in a global price-setting cartel despite the Islamic condemnation of monopolies?)

A similar ambivalence appears in the religions of the Asian world. Hindu and Buddhist traditions, for example, are noteworthy for their ability to include an extraordinarily wide range of beliefs and practices within their ambit of community. Yet Hindu nationalists in the Indian subcontinent have an undisguised antipathy toward Muslims and Christians within their midst. Even within the Hindu community itself, there is an "us and them" caste system, and the men who conceived of business as an *ashram* thought that it meant, among other things, giving preference to local suppliers rather than to imports.

In Buddhism, which is conceptually even more tolerant of diversity than Hinduism, there are exclusivist streams of thought such as Nichiren Buddhism. It proclaims the superiority of those devoted to a particular sacred text, the *Lotus Sutra.* Ambivalent attitudes toward others show up among people of Confucian background as well. While the highest Confucian ideal is the unity of heaven and all of humanity, this ideal is the outer ring of a series of concentric circles of relationships. The circles begin with the family, then community, then nation, and only gradually extend outward to world and, ultimately, to heaven.

The unwritten and unspoken bonds of trust among members of tightly knit Chinese business communities are readily observable. But it is far from clear that the same bonds of trust can exist in their dealings with, say, an American business. Even within a totally Chinese setting, moreover, some entities will be part of a common network while some will be outside the network. As one observer has said: "In a society in which the most fundamentally right thing to pursue is one's own family welfare, no assumptions can be made about the goodwill of others until the obligation bonds have been built."

Coming back to the case at hand, Al can indeed draw on religious ethical traditions to make a case for "America first" (or whatever community one is a part of). But I think that Rick could draw on these traditions to make a stronger case. The Confucian model of concentric circles is a good representation of the way most religions think about "the face of the other." The circles begin at home, but they branch out as each circle in turn satisfies its own needs. In a prosperous society such as ours, the workers in Al's and Rick's plants do have options. The export of American jobs is most unlikely to result in the dire consequences Al foresees.

But what of Al's sense that he and Rick would not only be transferring American jobs, but that the jobs would be going to countries that exploit children and are unconcerned about polluting the environment? Let's turn to those issues next.

Child Labor

> The parents of a child are but his enemies when they fail to educate him properly.
>
> *Hindu Garuda Purana 115*
>
> When Confucius was going to [the town of] Wei, Jan Chiu drove him. The Master said: "What a dense population!" Jan Chiu asked: "When the people have multiplied, what should be done for them?" The Master said: "Enrich them." Jan Chiu asked: "When

> one has enriched them, what next should be done for them?" The Master said: "Instruct them."
>
> *Analects 13:9*

Intense price competition in apparel, small plastic goods, and other industries with high labor content has led many U.S. manufacturers and retailers to use contractors in underdeveloped areas of the world where wages are low—in part because of the contractors' use of child labor. The International Labor Organization, an arm of the United Nations, has estimated that in 1995 about 120 million children between the ages of five and fourteen worked full-time and another 130 million worked part-time. About 60 percent of these 250 million working children were in Asia, 30 percent in Africa, and most of the rest in Latin America. The majority of the children were employed in agriculture or as domestic servants, but a large number worked in mines, construction, fishing, and a wide variety of factories—almost always in unsanitary and often hazardous surroundings.

Does this mean that the parents of these children love them less than American parents love their children or that they would not prefer that the children were in school rather than at work? That is very doubtful. As the first quotation indicates, even in ancient India parents had a strong responsibility to educate their children (at least their sons). Did nineteenth- and early-twentieth-century American parents whose children worked in often grisly factories love them less than today's American parents love their children?

It is a historical and sociological reality that until parents can, on their own, support their families, their children are put to work. The quotation from Confucius shows the priority: first enrich them, then instruct them. Furthermore, religious faith tends to inculcate a stoic acceptance of difficult circumstances that seem unable to be changed. Every religious community in every part of the world is concerned for the welfare of its children. But survival is also a religious value (as well as a biological one), and it usually transcends concerns about putting children to work.

Recognizing that it will be a long time, if ever, before the general level of worldwide affluence makes child labor unnecessary, many governmental, quasi-governmental, religious, and philanthropic groups have been working with socially responsible companies to develop minimal standards for child labor. The standards deal with minimum ages at which children may work in different occupations, maximum hours they may work, and the physical surroundings in which they work. Some voices in America, particularly trade union leaders, have called for punitive restrictions on trade in products made by children in violation of these standards. They would, in effect, prohibit imports of such products and, similarly, constrain the export of jobs to nations that do not comply with the standards.

The proponents of such import and export restrictions have generally been viewed by the nations of Asia, Africa, and Latin America as disingenuous. Even the labor unions of these nations, which regularly fight for higher wages and improved working conditions, see the efforts of their American counterparts as a disguised form of protectionism. The protection of American jobs, they feel, is what motivates proposals for import controls rather than the protection of foreign children and their families. The result, they say, is to hurt, not help, the foreign workers. Indeed, they point to America's lax enforcement of laws to protect workers in American sweatshops or migrant workers on American farms as evidence of disingenuousness.

Professor Jagdish Bhagwati, an Indian-born international trade expert who teaches at Columbia University, echoes this sentiment. He recently told a newspaper reporter that trading bans "may make your conscience look good but won't get desired results. The displaced child workers will not end up in school, where they belong, and may be forced into even more degrading labor, such as pornography and prostitution. We need a sophisticated solution that doesn't just rely on sanctions."

Janet's proposal to Al and Rick, in our case, might be an example of the kind of sophisticated solution that Professor Bhagwati has in mind. It is a proposal that recognizes the financial needs of running the business effectively while leaning toward Rick's interpretation of what his and Al's faith demands. Janet believes that the company can set an example of higher wages and better working conditions for children who might be employed in their foreign facilities. Unit labor costs would still be lower than in the United States, permitting the company to lower its prices to meet the competition. To be fully price competitive against producers who are more exploitive, profit margins would have to be reduced a bit, but not so much as to really hurt, according to her calculations.

Al thinks that it is naïve to believe that this example might, if publicized, actually increase their customer base. But Rick is willing to try and to make some personal financial sacrifice if it doesn't work out as he and Janet expect. Since Al is also willing to make a financial sacrifice to do the right thing, let's assume that he can be persuaded by Janet's proposal. Now, what about the environmental and gender issues raised by the case?

Environmental Ethics

As I've noted, people in poor countries often think that wealthy Westerners who want to boycott imports of products made with child labor are really protectionists hiding behind a cloak of concern for children. A similar suspicion has bogged down international discussions of environmental protection. Western nations demand stronger environmental regulations from the governments of Asia, Africa, and Latin America. They, in turn, argue that their relatively lower standards do not stem from a lesser concern about the issue but from a need for economic growth that forces environmental concerns to have lower priority.

Recent surveys of consumers in poor countries show a high degree of awareness of the health hazards of air and water pollution. Actually, it is a higher awareness than consumers in wealthy countries, probably because the latter have made more progress than the former in coming to grips with the problem. The surveys reinforce the claim of foreign governments that it is not lack of concern but lack of financial wherewithal that is holding them back. They are taking steps to protect the environment, they say, but only as fast as their financial resources allow; and this is no different from what happened in the economic history of the Western world.

The arguments of the less-developed countries (LDCs) are rather persuasive. Can anyone deny that the developed world's attention to the environment is of very recent origin? In fact, the Judeo-Christian tradition of the West has generally viewed nature as subordinate to human beings, in keeping with the hierarchy established in the biblical account of creation.

> God blessed [Adam and Eve] and said to them, Be fruitful and multiply; fill the earth and subdue it; and have dominion over the fish of the sea, the birds of the sky, and over every living thing that moves on the earth.
>
> *Genesis 1:28*

The *Qur'an* contains similar phraseology supporting the idea that humanity is the pinnacle of God's creative energies. To be sure, in all three Abrahamic traditions, human beings are said to be *trustees* of the material world that God created. But it is only recently that commentators have become convinced that an emphasis on the biblical words *subdue and have dominion over*—and similar words in the *Qur'an*—misconstrues the overall sense of the creation narratives. Such emphasis, for example, overlooks another divine ecological instruction in the Bible:

> If you besiege a town for a long time, making war against it in order to take it, you must not destroy its trees by wielding an ax against them. Although you may take food from them, you must not cut them down. Are trees in the fields human beings that they should come under siege from you?
>
> *Deuteronomy 20:19*

The modern commentators ask: If the natural environment must be protected even in times of war, how much more so does it need to be protected from everyday economic activity? Environment-friendly themes have been discovered not only in scripture but also in the folk stories and festivals of Jews, Christians, and Muslims. For example, Jamal Badawi, a Muslim scholar, interprets various sayings of Muhammad to be indicative of the Prophet's strong environmental concerns. These sayings include the importance of punishing "anyone who kills a sparrow without a legitimate reason," or "one who cuts a tree for no good reason," or one who uses "an excessive amount of water to make ablution in preparation for prayers." (Badawi's discussion appears on pp. 306–7 of *Spiritual Goods*, an anthology of essays on religious ethics of business edited by Stewart W. Herman.) I submit, however, that these pro-ecology text discoveries and interpretations are so recent as to suggest that they reflect a great deal of ex post facto "reading in" of environmental concerns to a history that was, in fact, not so concerned. Let me give some illustrations.

The history of Jewish jurisprudence indicates that antipollution concerns need to be balanced against the economic costs of pollution control. Take, for example, cases involving the protection of the community against noxious side effects of otherwise legitimate commercial activity. First, plaintiffs had to demonstrate a close link between the noxious situation and the commercial activity they alleged to have caused the condition. Second, the noxious situation had to cause serious harm, not just unpleasantness or inconvenience. Finally, the judges deciding the case had to weigh the harm to the plaintiffs against the economic damage the defendant would suffer by preventing or removing his noxious-causing activity.

Catholic environmentalism is also of fairly recent origin. For example, in *Centesimus Annus*, issued in 1991, Pope John Paul II expresses concern about environmental destruction. Yet he acknowledges that in early stages of economic development people have always "lived under the weight of necessity." "The ecological question," he says, "accompanies the problem of consumerism." Of course, the less developed areas of the world are not immune from consumerism, but the overall thrust of the pope's environmental concern is directed to those who have achieved a high level of affluence.

Similarly, the Protestant "social gospel" was mainly directed at alleviating human poverty. It is only rather recently that Protestant social pronouncements have been heavily directed to ecological concerns. Here, the biblical notion of trusteeship, or stewardship, has been strongly emphasized.

One of my teachers, Max Stackhouse, believes that the word *stewardship* comes from Old English and reflects the appointment of highly reliable workers to be wardens of the pigsty, or *sty-wards*. These wardens, says Stackhouse, "living under the 'word' of the 'lord' of the manor, were to become trustworthy custodians of those resources that were indispensable to the life and well-being of the whole community." Putting the idea of stewardship into a theological context, Stackhouse says that all people are God's stewards and, as such, are entrusted to care for the material, as well as the human, resources of God's world.

It is noteworthy that the homebuilder I cited in chapter 3 was concerned not only with the suitability of his houses for the people who will live in them. He was concerned, as well, with the resource efficiency of his construction techniques. Businesspeople, both Protestants and others, who have taken to heart the modern version of the stewardship concept are deeply concerned about environmental degradation. It is noteworthy that a group of timber companies have formed what they call the *Forest Stewardship Council*. Its goal is to establish standards of environmentally sound logging practices and to appoint inspectors to certify whether any given timber operation has met the standards. If the operation is so certified, products made with that timber could be specially labeled for the information of consumers. A similar organization is being put together in the fishing industry, called the *Marine Stewardship Council*.

The *Harvard Business Review* has reported a significant trend among large corporations to issue detailed public reports on their environmental performance. But it should be noted that these are very recent developments. They could not have been imagined even a few decades ago in the United States, much less when industrialization was just beginning. So why should we expect severely underdeveloped areas of the world to give environmental concerns high priority?

The religious traditions of the East give no more support for environmental activism when people are going hungry than do the traditions of the Western world. Confucianism is certainly humanity-centered rather than nature-centered; and while Hinduism is more nature-oriented than Confucianism, its stoic view of life does not urge environmental activism when so many Hindus are starving.

Buddhism is, in theory at least, the most environment-conscious religion of Asia and Africa. The "do no harm" requirement of "right livelihood" suggests that the modern ecological movement probably would have resonated with the Buddha. It seems reasonable to assume that Buddhist convictions about the interrelatedness of everything provide strong grounds for interpreting rather broadly the injunction against economic activity that is harmful. While it clearly should not be harmful to *people*, it probably should not be harmful to the *environment* either. Nevertheless, neither the Buddha nor his disciples, even up to the modern era, had much to say on the subject. Thus, if Western religious thinking has become significantly concerned with environmental ethics only as Western affluence has expanded, it is hardly surprising that the peoples of Asia, Africa, and Latin America have been slower to take up the cause.

Let me turn now to the final ethical issue raised in our case. Setting up plants in Asia would mean that Janet, as Chief Operating Officer, would be walking into a world of male chauvinism far more intense than anything she is likely to have experienced heretofore.

Women in the Global Workplace

> Women and servants are most difficult to deal with.
> If you are familiar with them, they cease to be humble.
> If you keep a distance from them, they resent it.
>
> *Analects 17:25*

If truth be told, this saying of Confucius reflected not only his own attitude toward women, but it is not too different from the attitude of most religious traditions, of both the East and the West. Most have suppressed the voices of women in their texts and their leadership. Changes are under way, but the rate of change is slow, particularly in areas of the world that are the target locales of job exports.

There are some real ironies in the male chauvinism of the world's religions. First, women have done much to sustain the health and vigor of the very traditions that have treated them so poorly. Second, it was not always the case that religions viewed women as second-class citizens. In many instances, the original foundations of the religious traditions were quite egalitarian.

In primitive societies, women were often held in as high esteem as men, and sometimes higher. The history of ancient Israel, for example, included the veneration of goddesses such as Asherah, Ishtar, and Anat, especially among the women of the Israelite tribes; and this continued for a considerable time after the Revelation at Sinai. Moreover, though the biblical redactors endowed the One God with essentially masculine characteristics, a fairly strong feminine side of divinity was maintained. God's spirit is described both in the Bible and in the dialogues of the rabbis as the *shekhina*, a term of female gender. Similarly in Islam, while *al-Lah*, or *Allah*, is a noun of masculine gender, the Arabic word for the inscrutable essence of God is a feminine term, *al-Dhat*. In the Orient, likewise, the divine pantheon of the Hindus has always included many goddesses.

It is true, of course, that biblical Israel, like most ancient societies, was patriarchal. Yet the matriarchs of the Bible were clearly forceful women who participated fully with their husbands in the shaping of their families' major decisions. While they did it in a way that allowed their men to feel that they had the final say, the Bible does not hide the pretense factor. Biblical figures such as Ruth and Esther are further examples of nonservile women; and some women, like Deborah, actually led armies of men into battle. But as time went on, Jewish religious and communal life became managed almost entirely by the rabbis, and women were not permitted to enter that charmed circle. Yes, the rabbis loved and treasured their wives and daughters, but the female role was confined almost entirely to the home. In recent decades, thankfully, this role has been greatly expanded, especially in non-Orthodox circles.

The male takeover of Christian and Islamic religious society was, in a sense, even more dramatic than in Judaism. Women were strongly attracted to early Christian groups by pronouncements such as Saint Paul's to the Galatian community.

> There is no longer Jew or Greek; there is no longer slave or free;
> there is no longer male or female; for all of you are one in Christ Jesus.
>
> *Galatians 3:28*

Yet subsequent letters to other new Christian communities, although attributed to Paul but mainly written by his disciples, recontextualized Paul's words. They placed his ideas about men and women within so-called household codes that required the submission of wives to their husbands. To be sure, Christian husbands were commanded to love their wives and, like the Jewish rabbis, undoubtedly did. But the societal roles of women were marginalized, a condition that was reinforced by the later writings of Saint Augustine, who viewed sexuality as the source of original sin and equated all women with "Eve the temptress." In many ways, broad swaths of Christian life even up to our day have been tainted by the Augustinian attitude.

In Islam, women were prominent among Muhammad's early converts, as he denounced their inferior role in Arabic tribal life. In fact, before his revelations began Muhammad was a merchant in the employ of a woman, and she earned his deep respect. The *Qur'an* addresses women's issues frequently and sympathetically. For example, it prohibits the tribal custom of female infanticide, and it gives women previously withheld legal rights, such as inheritance and divorce.

Significantly, female veiling was initially prescribed only for Muhammad's wives, and that as a status symbol. But in the years following Muhammad's death, men co-opted the veil, both metaphorically and operationally. Men made the veil not a symbol of status but of subordination and seclusion from public society. In our day, Muslim feminists not only are discarding the veil but are also calling for a return to the intentions of Muhammad.

Turning to the religious traditions of the East, I have already indicated that the preeminent figure in what we call Confucianism was either a misogynist or close to it. In Chinese culture, therefore, the subservient role of women was not a change but a continuation. That is not the case, however, in Hindu tradition.

The ancient Vedas suggest that the status of women once was considerably higher than it came to be in later generations. Young girls, for example, apparently were required to receive instruction in the hymns along with their brothers. The hymns themselves, moreover, extol female as well as male paradigms. Somehow this perception of women changed, however, and later epic poems of Hindu tradition portray them as lying, vicious, and needing to be controlled by their husbands. Perhaps the most dramatic manifestation of the subordinate status of Hindu women, illegal for many years yet still practiced in some villages, is the *sati*, the immolation of widows in the cremation fires of their husbands. On the other hand, it must be recognized that side by side with the subordination of women since the days of the ancient Vedas is the phenomenon of several politically powerful women who have rallied the spirits of Hindu feminists. They hold out the possibility of major reform during the years ahead.

In Buddhist tradition as well, women are respected but subordinate to men. A story is told in which the Buddha was advising a young wife whose family was complaining about her arrogance. The Buddha told her that there are seven types of wives. One is "like a murderer": she dishonors her husband and her heart turns to another man. A second is "like a thief," wasting her husband's income on luxuries. A third is "like a master," neglecting the housekeeping and always scolding her husband. Fourth, there is the wife who is "like a mother," caring for her husband as she would her child. A fifth type of wife is "like a sister," faithful to her husband and serving him with modesty. Sixth is the wife who is "like a friend": she tries to please her husband as if he were a friend returned from a long absence. Finally, there is a wife who is "like a maid-servant," respecting her husband, obeying his commands, and having no wishes of her own. The young woman then regretted her past behavior and the Buddha asked her which of the seven types of wife she would now want to become. "The one in the last example, the maid-servant," she replied.

Has the model of the submissive woman changed since the Buddha's day? A bit, but not much, from what I have been able to discern. I find it quite interesting, for example, that a book entitled *Engaged Buddhism*, and subtitled *Buddhist Liberation Movements in Asia*, has fairly lengthy commentary on the growing role of women in Buddhist religious orders but virtually nothing on women in the workplace.

I think I've said enough by now to make clear the challenge that Janet will have to confront if her company sets up facilities in Asia in which she will be in charge. Her situation reminds me of a woman I know of who transitioned from theologian to bank executive. She believes that women need to see themselves in multiple roles and that it might actually be sinful to make one role the center of life to the exclusion of others. Thus, she says, a posture of total self-sacrifice by a woman to the care of her family "can become sinful if it reflects a fundamental lack of self-love and a desire to be seen as righteous." Similarly, a woman may be acting sinfully if she identifies herself exclusively with her career and sets aside the needs of her family.

The challenge for Janet, in our case, is not career versus family. Rather, it is her own managerial role versus the psychic needs of the men she will have to supervise. Her comments to Al and Rick suggest that she understands the need to see herself in multiple roles. She will not give up her role as the supervisor of the men; but she will carry out that role in a way that respects the sensitivities of those men and of the culture in which they were raised.

Janet's approach can, of course, be carried to an unhealthy extreme. For example, the *Wall Street Journal* recently ran a story that told how a female export manager of an American brewing company turned a blind eye to the use by its "independent" Asian distributor of "beer girls"—a euphemism for you-know-what-kind of girls—to promote its brands in Cambodia. The article quoted the president of the company as saying "I'm not in charge of the morality of these countries, and even if I were, I couldn't change it." No, but he could change his distributor, couldn't he?

Surely there are many opportunities for business firms to foster greater respect for women in societies where they are poorly treated. Yet Janet's balanced approach might be commended not only to women in the workplace but to all people who have to confront the challenges of clashing cultures—the challenges of confronting "the face of the other"—in an expanding global marketplace.

PART IV

GETTING FROM HERE TO THERE

To borrow a phrase from my discussion of Islam, I have argued that the marketplace is not just an economic sphere; "it is a region of the human spirit." Self-interest is, to be sure, an aspect of the human spirit that drives the decisions most of us make every day in the marketplace. But those decisions also have significant moral content, because each decision we make affects not only ourselves but other human beings as well—and often the animal and natural world in addition. To the extent that our economic decisions impact others, we have a moral responsibility to assess our self-interest in the context of our broader sense of right and wrong.

The human sense of right and wrong reflects a complex interweaving of nature and nurture. Not least of the nurturing factors is the religious teaching that most people in the world absorb, consciously or subconsciously. Consequently, it is important to learn about the ethical teachings of the world's great religious traditions to see what they have to say about behavior in the marketplace. Indeed, even totally secular people can learn a great deal from the accumulated wisdom of thousands of years of religious thinking about economic behavior.

While each of the six religious traditions I have studied has a stream of thought that is strongly otherworldly (some more so than others), each also has a stream of practical "this-worldliness." I have reviewed the ways that the scriptures, sages, and communal traditions of these religions have sought to bring their sense of the sacred to the everyday world of commercial activity. Now it is time to sum up and consider next steps.

I have three goals for this final part of my book. First, I want to show how broad a range of agreement there is among the various religious communities about ethics in the marketplace. Second, I want to consider various reasons why these ideas about right and wrong behavior are so often violated. Third, I want to suggest some steps that might help to close the gap.

9

Ideals and Obstacles

Is does not imply ought;
but ought implies can.

THIS TWO-PART APHORISM of moral philosophy sounds complicated but really isn't. The first part means simply that the way we actually behave is not necessarily—indeed, all too frequently is not—the way we ought to behave. That, after all, is what moral ideals are about. In the first section of this chapter, I will pull together the teachings of the great religions about how, ideally, we ought and ought not to behave in the marketplace.

The second part of the aphorism points out that moral ideals mean little unless there is reason to hope that what *ought* to be *can* be. It is futile to tell people that they ought to do, or refrain from doing, something that their circumstances really do not permit. On the other hand, moral ideals challenge us to rethink what we can or cannot do. It is all too easy to think that our circumstances are so special that the moral ideals place unrealistic demands on us. These perceptions are the subject of the second section of the chapter.

AN ETHICAL CONSENSUS

The broad ethical themes of the great religions that I described in part II, together with the concrete case discussions in part III, indicate that there is a considerable range of agreement on how people should and should not behave in the marketplace. I would put this consensus into operational terms as follows.

Selling and Buying

All merchants need to put their best foot forward, but deceit is something else. Deceitful merchants violate a buyer's person as well as his or her purse. Therefore,

Sellers should not

- present their goods or services as having highly favorable characteristics that they do not have, or
- withhold significant negative information that a buyer cannot readily discover.

In the spirit of reciprocity,

- Buyers should not mislead sellers about their intentions. (Note: In most traditions, this responsibility is more implicit than explicit. Moreover, it is becoming less relevant in a world of electronic commerce.)

In the interests of communal harmony, health, and well-being,

Sellers should not

- maliciously disparage competitors or their products in advertising or other sales messages,
- offer products to buyers who are likely to use them in a manner harmful to themselves or to others,
- engage in tactics that artificially raise the prices of goods essential to the preservation of life or reduce their availability,
- produce or distribute their products in ways that damage the natural environment. (Note: This caveat is of fairly recent vintage in religious history, and its application is often contingent on a community's stage of economic development.)

Professional Ethics

Professionals who are in special positions of trust have responsibilities that transcend those of ordinary merchants. Therefore,

Medical, legal, financial, and other such professionals

- should not imply that they have skills that they do not have,
- should present clients with alternative courses of action, and
- should disclose potential conflicts of interest.
- Members of corporate Boards of Directors have a moral obligation to bring the interests of the larger society to bear on the organization's business decisions.

- Bribery is unethical.
- Lenders should be willing to suspend their rights under civil law to assist borrowers in distress.

Ethics in the Workplace

Employers and employees need to bargain from their own vantage points. But workers should not be treated as just another commodity in the marketplace. Among other things, this means:

- Workers should participate in the structuring of their jobs.
- Layoffs, when necessary, should be made with advance notice, and transitional assistance should be provided.
- Management should not show partiality among employees of different rank when judging and punishing infractions.
- Child labor should be avoided. If necessary for a community's economic survival, it should be accompanied by special efforts to maintain healthful working conditions and limit the number of hours worked.
- Women and men in the workplace are equally deserving of human dignity and respect, whether they are supervisors or rank-and-file workers. (Note: Issues such as child labor and environmental degradation have evoked a great deal of controversy, but the disputes are not as much about ultimate goals as they are about the rate of progress toward the goals. However, on gender issues there are intense interreligious and intrareligious disputes about ultimate goals—that is, about whether women and men have inherently different roles to play in society. Given this lack of consensus, perhaps the best approach would be reflected in Janet's behavior in the case involving a transfer of jobs from the United States to Asia. Recall that she refused to relinquish her supervisory role but was prepared to carry out that role in a way that respects the sensitivities of the men she would be supervising. Hopefully, the day will come when those men will be equally conscious of female sensitivities.)

A noteworthy aspect of my statement of ethical consensus is the preponderance of "should nots" compared with "shoulds." It has been my experience that the negative versions of many ethical ideas are usually easier to understand and apply to practical situations than the positive versions. For example, "tell the truth" leaves open the question of how much detail is necessary. It is a judgment call as to which details are significant in any given situation and which are not. Moreover, telling the whole truth is sometimes harmful. When you try to comfort someone who has lost a loved one, for instance, you go out of your way to say something nice about the deceased even though he or she may have had a great many failings. In other words, "white lies" often foster good human relationships. Consequently, "do not intentionally mislead an innocent party" can be a far more practical guide to ethical behavior than "tell the truth."

I recently was discussing my research with a Protestant minister. He referred to my fondness for "should nots" as a "negative ethic," and he asked me whether such an approach is really satisfactory. "Satisfactory to whom," I asked. "To God," he answered. His response left me rather troubled. Surely it is vital that clergymen and women challenge us to be proactively ethical. But maximalist demands can boomerang. People may simply turn off their hearing aids.

Admittedly, an ethic that challenges us to proactively help others sets a more noble standard than a "negative ethic" that insists that we do no harm to others. But "do not hurt" stands a much better chance of being broadly understood and achieved, if only because it involves less self-sacrifice. I believe that the British ethicist Sir Geoffrey Vickers was on to something important when he said, in *Value Systems and Social Process* (p. 116):

> I believe that most regulative behaviour is negative, the avoidance of some relation which has been defined as unacceptable. Even the most positive aspirations of governments may be so regarded. The welfare legislation of my own country is based on a report which identified "five giant evils." The whole of human progress may be convincingly described as successive redefinings of the unacceptable.

What's Getting in the Way?

Whether I focus on the "should nots" or my minister friend focuses on the "shoulds," either way it is painfully obvious that most people's actual behavior in the marketplace falls far short of the religious consensus I've described. Is this because most people are basically immoral? Maybe, but I think not.

In the preface of this book I spoke about my own company's ethical failing. Large numbers of its sales agents had misled their clients. While I was not directly involved in the marketing area of the company, I knew many of the people involved. I was struck by the fact that most of the sales agents, and most of the sales executives who looked the other way, were solid citizens in their nonbusiness activities. They were churchgoing people with strong family and community ties. I myself fit that description, yet I had been guilty of verbally abusing subordinates.

It is apparent to even the most casual observer that people do things in their business lives that they would not dream of doing in their personal lives. This ethical schizophrenia has been explained in various ways. The first is reflected in the evolution of economic theory that I described in chapter 1. There I showed that whereas Adam Smith considered economics to be a branch of moral philosophy, most of his successors accepted the doctrine of the economic man. This doctrine says, in effect, that it is natural for people to bifurcate their ethical lives. People know that consciously moral behavior is expected of them in their personal lives but consider the world of business to be an *amoral* realm. It's not that they deliberately set out to do unethical things in the marketplace but rather that ethical considerations do not seem particularly relevant. The goal is to maximize material well-being and minimize material costs. Archie B. Carroll, a professor of management who has written widely on business ethics, calls this attitude "intentional amorality."

It is noteworthy that Carroll's own experience as a business consultant leads him to conclude that there really are not many people who fit the description of the intentionally amoral economic man. Rather, what he has observed is "unintentional amorality." In a recent article entitled "Ethical Challenges for Business in the New Millennium," he asserts that most business managers "are well-intentioned but are self-centered in the sense that they do not possess the ethical perception, awareness, or discernment to realize that many of their decisions, actions, policies, and behaviors have an ethical facet or dimension that is being overlooked." Unintentionally amoral managers, he says, "pursue profitability within the confines of the letter of the law, as they do not think about the spirit of the law. They do not perceive who might be hurt by their actions."

Tom Morris is a philosopher who wrote a best-selling book with the catchy title *If Aristotle Ran General Motors*. Morris does not use the term *unintentional amorality*, but he has observed a similar phenomenon during the course of his years as a business consultant. In fact, he admits that he himself has often been prone to that kind of inattention to the moral consequences of his behavior—even in his personal life, moreover. He tells of "a moral audit" he did of his life, and of his surprise at the results. Morris had compiled a list of things he had done that he later recognized as ethically wrong. He searched for a common denominator and concluded that in every case he had failed to perceive the full consequences of his actions for other people as well as for himself.

So we now have three possible reasons why people behave badly in the marketplace: (1) they are intentionally immoral; (2) they are intentionally amoral; and (3) they are unintentionally amoral. I'd like to add a fourth possibility, one that I think explains my own ethical lapses in business (and often in personal matters, as well) and the ethical lapses I have observed in many others. I'll call it "moral but with excuses." It's analogous to the plea one often hears in traffic court: "Guilty, Your Honor, but with an explanation."

Moral reasoning, whether religious or secular or a combination thereof, rarely requires a person to be a hero. Indeed, we honor heroes and call some people "saintly" precisely because they have acted in a way that most people cannot be expected to act. I, and most people I know, would like to abide by the kinds of ethical principles I outlined a few pages back. But we frequently feel that the competitive circumstances of the moment don't allow us to.

Consider, for example, my business colleagues who engaged in misleading sales practices. They were commission salesmen and women who needed to generate sales in order to put food on the family table. Moreover, the bonuses of their supervisors were also dependent on those sales. There is enormous pressure for commission salespeople to be less than totally honest with clients and to rationalize what are, in fact, unethical sales practices by saying to themselves, "If I don't do it, someone else will."

To take another example, the economic survival of the leaders of a business requires that they produce competitive rates of return on the capital invested in their businesses. This is especially true of the leaders in publicly owned corporations, as opposed to people who run their own business outright and can, if they wish, be content with lesser rates of return. William Clay Ford, Chairman of Ford Motor Company, great-grandson of Henry Ford, made this point vividly in a meeting with newspaper reporters. He acknowledged that the company's most profitable products, its sport utility vehicles (SUVs), do not meet the company's own goals for social responsibility, particularly in the area of tailpipe emissions. He said that the company was doing many things to make its SUV emissions even less than allowed by law, but that he didn't have anywhere near the free hand his great-grandfather had when he owned the whole company. The younger Ford was not implying that his ancestor had been a model of a socially responsible manager but rather that he could make decisions without the difficulties of "persuading Wall Street that it was worthwhile for Ford Motor to take big steps to be perceived as progressive and environmentally friendly."

Next, suppose that ABC Corp. and XYZ Inc. are *both* publicly owned corporations. And suppose that XYZ frequently uses inexpensive production techniques that tend to pollute the environment—although not so much as to run afoul of antipollution laws. ABC's management might have higher ethical standards and want to go beyond the letter of the law, but they are under enormous competitive pressure to relax those standards in order to survive. They may know what they ought to do, but feel that they can't.

The trend toward globalization of business has exacerbated these problems of ought versus can. The term *globalization* does not refer only to the fact that economic activity occurs across national borders. There is nothing very new about that. What globalization means, more significantly, is that the economic system of the whole world is becoming a single competitive marketplace. It is not only competitive, but fiercely so, with product life cycles becoming ever shorter and pressures to cut costs relentless. These pressures tend to push ethics to the back burner when business decisions have to be made. Joseph Badaracco has framed the dilemma well in his book *Defining Moments: When Managers Must Choose between Right and Right*. He says (pp. 119–120): "Managers live and work in two worlds simultaneously. One is a web of responsibilities, commitments, and ethical aspirations. . . . The other is an arena of intense, sometimes brutal competition."

Nor are consumers exempt from the same sorts of ethical pressures. People of modest means feel that they must buy their staple goods at the lowest available prices. Now, suppose that one provider of children's footwear sells sneakers cheaply because his factories are located in countries where poor working conditions are customary. Low-income consumers are under great pressure to buy those sneakers for their children rather than the more expensive ones of a producer who treats his workers better. They may well have ethical qualms about it, yet feel they have no choice given their financial circumstances.

Even when economic survival is not at stake, pressures against ethical behavior often are generated by a need to make choices in a group context. A manager usually is only one of many managers in a firm. A salesperson usually is only one of many. And a consumer often goes shopping with friends—or at least talks to them about the purchases they are making. D. Don Welch has addressed the issue of group decision making in a book called *Conflicting Agendas*.

"We are a part of institutions that exert enormous pressures on us in molding our conduct," Welch writes (pp. 2–4), "but the conduct they would mold is often not the conduct we would otherwise choose for ourselves." It is not a matter of acting as a group member on one occasion and as my "real self" on another, he continues. "My 'real self' comes out of those groups to which I belong. My perspective on the world, the information that is available to me, and the way I respond to those realities are all influenced by my situation within larger social bodies. Thus in a sense the conflicts we experience are not those between a personal self and a social self, but between different social selves."

There is no reason to assume that the balance of pressures on a person's "different social selves" will push toward exemplary ethical behavior. It is very difficult to swim against the tide. As individuals, we may know what we ought to do. But can we, when the group acts otherwise?

My own life's experience tells me that sometimes we really can't. We would have to be heroes to act the way we ought to. But an honest examination of my life's experience also tells me that the argument "Everybody's doing it, so I also have to" is too often a mere rationalization for taking the easy way out.

Wanted: Moral Managers or Moral Markets?

In 1999, John R. Boatright delivered the presidential address to the Society for Business Ethics, one of the preeminent associations of university professors of business ethics. In his speech, Boatright undertook an evaluation of the successes and failures of this academic field during the previous twenty-five years. He noted with great pride a huge growth in the number of business ethics courses in colleges, a profusion of books on the subject, countless articles in both academic and trade journals, and an unending round of ethics seminars and conferences all over the world. Yet Boatright observed, sadly, that despite all of this intellectual attention to business ethics, in actual practice "the reports from the field are not encouraging."

Boatright urged his listeners to rethink what it is they are trying to achieve, noting that he had rethought his own ideas and come to a new understanding. Most business ethicists, he said, have focused on developing "moral managers," meaning managers who not only *act* morally but who *think* morally. The moral manager is one "who actually includes moral considerations in business decision making." This effort to develop moral managers, Boatright had now concluded, has been a mistake. He offered several reasons why ethicists would be fighting a losing battle if they continued along the same path. Some of his reasons are similar to the ones I've been discussing.

First, he observed, the effort to develop moral managers has been directed mainly at Chief Executive Officers of large corporations. The assumption has been that these people would set an example that would filter down and throughout their organizations—particularly because moral CEOs would run participatory companies in which rank-and-file workers would have a voice in decisions affecting them. The problem with this assumption, Boatright had now concluded, was that the most admired CEOs—in fact, those most rewarded by the stock market—are "hard-headed, business-savvy decision makers." Not only are they hard-headed; they do not encourage broad-based participation in business decisions.

Another problem with the focus on corporate CEOs, according to Boatright, is that most people in business are followers, not leaders. Most employees work in small and mid-sized firms, in government, and in non-profit institutions. The moral-managers approach, he had decided, "does not speak to their situation."

Furthermore, he continued, people in the marketplace are not only producers and sellers of goods and services; they have other roles as well. Most importantly, they are consumers; and consumers, he says, including himself, usually behave as the classical economic man. They seek the best prices; not the most ethical vendors.

If the "Moral Manager Model" is a mistake, Boatright asked his audience rhetorically, what is the alternative? His answer was to focus attention on the market mechanism itself rather than on the individuals who operate in it. "Many ethical problems," he said, "arise from market and regulatory failures." Hence, he proposed a "Moral Market Model," whose goal would be to "create more efficient markets and more effective regulation."

If this goal were achieved, individual responsibility would have limited scope. As Boatright put it, "instead of 'Increase responsibility,' the motto of the Moral Market Model might be 'Reduce options.'"

As an example of what he had in mind, Boatright cited with approval the Federal Sentencing Guidelines, which classify various levels of business criminality and prescribe mandatory punishments for each level. These legal requirements, he said, create an incentive for people to behave ethically. As another example, he cited arrangements in which precise contracts spell out the terms of business relationships rather than relying on mutual trust.

Now, John R. Boatright is not a man whose views should be quickly dismissed. No lightweight or casual thinker delivers a presidential address to the Society for Business Ethics. Yet his arguments do strike me as flawed in several respects.

First, he seems to equate "hard-headed, business-savvy" decision making with unethical decision making, and I do not think the evidence necessarily supports that claim. Just as there are many scoundrels whose companies are highly valued in the stock market, there are other corporate senior managers who *think ethically*, as well as behave ethically, whose stocks carry high price-earnings ratios. My case examples in the preceding chapters tried to demonstrate that hard-headed decisions can take into account both ethics and bottom-line profitability.

Second, Boatright is quite correct that most businesspeople are not corporate CEOs. But as far as I can tell, this observation simply indicts business schools for training people to be something that most will never be. It doesn't indict the "Moral Manager Model," in my view; it calls for a redefinition of who the moral managers of economic life should be—the followers as well as the leaders.

Similarly, there is no logical reason why business schools—indeed, why all schools, beginning with kindergarten—should not teach people to be moral consumers as well as moral managers. Surely the recent success of nongovernmental anti-sweatshop organizations in mobilizing consumer sentiment is indicative that consumers are not impervious to moral appeals, even at the expense of their purely monetary interests. In fact, the amazing growth of the Internet has made rapid and widespread dissemination of information about antisocial behavior a major tool for bringing ethical considerations to bear on consumer decisions.

As for more effective regulation of markets, I believe that the process of globalization makes civil law a less reliable tool rather than a more reliable one. There are no global legislative and enforcement bodies, and international treaties among governments are as often obeyed in the breach as adhered to. But even if improved legislation and regulation were an answer, I fail to see why it is necessary to choose between a Moral Manager Model and a Moral Market Model. Striving to develop moral managers and moral consumers does not obviate the need for laws and regulations. Even the most ardent exponents of virtue ethics in the religious traditions I've reviewed in this book recognized that exclusive reliance on individual virtue is not wise. Laws are needed as well.

This latter observation brings me to my most serious critique of Boatright's analysis—and of all commentators who, in one way or another, give up hope that individual actors in the economic marketplace might be persuaded to behave more ethically, despite the many obstacles. In my opinion, the pessimists have completely ignored the possibility that courses, books, articles, and seminars on business ethics do not address the most important source of most people's understanding of right and wrong. That understanding, by and large, does not come from reading Aristotle's *Nicomachean Ethics*, nor Kant's *Metaphysics of Morals*, nor from any other purely intellectual/philosophical treatise or discourse. Rather, it comes from most people's religious traditions.

Most business ethics courses, books, articles, and seminars do a pretty good job of showing how reason can be brought to bear on the ethical dilemmas of economic life, but they are less than convincing about *why we ought to behave well.* In the corporate world, for example, the title of Ethics Officer, virtually unknown fifteen years ago, has become quite common. In fact, there is an Ethics Officer Association whose membership has been booming—from a handful at its inception in 1992 to over seven hundred a decade later. Yet discussions among the members of the association and at the corporate ethics seminars they promote focus most heavily on legal requirements, on the utilitarian needs of society for honest enterprises, on the satisfaction derived from ethical teamwork, and even on possible financial rewards from doing the right thing. The more intellectually curious members discuss ethics as a philosophical discipline. These are all worthwhile discussions, to be sure; but they lack the sense of compelling urgency that religious thinking can offer.

The obstacles to economic morality have not emerged only recently. While the forces of globalization have doubtless exacerbated them, they are challenges as old as organized society. Business ethicists have tried to apply the teachings of Aristotle, Kant, and other great philosophers and social scientists to these problems. But purely intellectual exercises rarely bestir action. What business ethicists have generally failed to do is direct attention to how the sages of the world's religious traditions have tried to cope with analogous challenges. They have failed to tap into the deep well of ancient yet eternal values that most people in the world absorb with their mother's milk—but are not taught to apply to the world of business.

10

Next Steps

It is not your obligation to complete the task but you are not at liberty to desist from starting it.

THIS SAYING FROM the Jewish *Ethics of the Fathers* (2:21) has its counterpart in other religious traditions. People of faith cannot hope to perfect the world, but they are obliged to try to make it better. The economic marketplace is an important sphere of the world, and it is so far from being ethically perfect that no person of faith is at liberty to desist from trying to improve it.

There is a common notion that if you want to maintain a friendship with someone, it is best not to talk about religion with that person unless you are pretty sure that you have similar views to begin with. Some believe that this advice is particularly applicable in the business world. For example, in chapter 2, I referred to a study of attitudes toward spirituality in the workplace. Ian I. Mitroff and Elizabeth A. Denton, the researchers who conducted the study, reported that many people wish there were more opportunities to express their spiritual feelings in the workplace. But they hesitate to do so because they fear that "spiritual talk" can easily become "religious talk" that would offend their peers.

The clear and growing desire of working people to have greater opportunities for spiritual expression while on the job has struck a responsive chord in many companies. Indeed, federal law requires "reasonable accommodation" of religious practice in the workplace. So most companies provide flexible time schedules to permit religious observances. Some facilitate prayer breakfasts and spiritual retreats. Others allow for prayer breaks during the course of the day and provide prayer rooms for the purpose. Some companies are even hiring on-site chaplains, much as they provide other counseling services to employees.

Yet, as one observer puts it, "many firms treat religion in the workplace the way they treat sexual activity in the workplace; they ban it." Their reasoning is reflected in the responses given to Mitroff and Denton. When the subjects of their inquiry thought about organizations that are overtly spiritual, "a rigid and stereotypical image along the following lines often emerged: a spiritual organization is one in which a person is under tremendous pressure to accept the tenets of a particular faith or religion. Notably, too, whether the particular religion pictured is Christian, Hindu, Jewish, or Muslim, it is almost always perceived in highly fundamentalist terms" (p. 59). Consequently, "the vast majority of respondents felt that it was highly desirable to set clear limits on religious expression and talk in the workplace. Many felt even more strongly that zero-based tolerance policies should be set. In other words, no religious talk at all should be tolerated" (p. 73).

It is not only in the workplace where these attitudes prevail. One can find it in labor unions, in social organizations, in government, even in interfaith study groups and among members of a family. So if, as I believe, it is important for religious views to be brought to bear on ethical discussions, ways have to be found for people of faith to express those views in a fashion that is honest yet does not appear to be threatening or proselytizing.

It is interesting to note that while many of the interviewees I just referred to were nervous about even using the word *spirituality* in open discussion, an even larger proportion of the group "felt strongly that to avoid using the 'S-words' is a moral cop-out. They felt that unless one faces the phenomenon of spirituality and soul head on, one is prone to moral relativism, as in 'all values are equally good unless they hurt someone.' Moral relativism, in turn, was seen as leading to even more fads and gimmicks. 'Call it like it is and deal with it directly' was a common sentiment, expressed again and again" (p. vii).

How curious that they want to deal with "S-words" but not "R-words." In these respondents' minds, religion is associated with fundamentalism whereas spirituality is not. Spirituality connotes moral values to them, and they want to speak of those values. But religion connotes ideology to them, and they want that to remain in the private sphere. Yet most of the greatest spiritual personalities in human history were also religious personalities who cared deeply about moral values. Clearly, the challenge is not how to go about speaking spiritually but not religiously. More often than not, the two go hand in hand. The challenge is how to speak either spiritually or religiously without offending listeners who have different orientations.

I believe that there are a number of keys to nonthreatening religious discourse in groups where there is a diversity of religious backgrounds and views. First and foremost, any member of the group should feel free to say to another, "that kind of talk makes me uncomfortable." In this way, religious discourse would be taking a cue from the best in modern male–female relationships. It has become quite appropriate, for example, for a woman to say to a man who gives her a friendly kiss on the cheek, "I value your friendship, but I'd rather you not express it that way."

Religious dialogue would also be easier, I think, if members of the group assumed from the outset that metaphysical assertions are likely to cause discomfort to some in the group. For example, I doubt that anyone in an interfaith group would have a problem with someone saying, "Jesus urged us to love even our enemies." On the other hand, it would be insensitive to say within an interfaith group, "Jesus Christ is Lord and Savior." People who are not Christians can hardly be expected to feel at ease with that assertion.

Similarly, it would be quite acceptable for someone to say, "Confucius was more concerned about human behavior than about the spirit world." But to say "Confucius was an atheist" would be needlessly provocative unless the group was actually having a discussion of the meaning of theism, atheism, and agnosticism. In that case, comments about Confucius's attitudes toward the gods could be appropriate.

The normal courtesies of all sincere dialogue should apply also to religious discourse. Thus, it is unacceptably discourteous for someone to say, "That's a stupid idea" or "That's just wrong," rather than "I simply cannot agree with you on that." Moreover, people with particularly strong theological views would be well advised to discipline themselves to spend more time listening than speaking. Only in that way can they come to understand the sensitivities of the other members of the group, allay their anxieties, and judge the best way to state a position.

Finally, I would suggest that the main goal of interfaith ethical discourse should be to affect ways of thinking rather than to develop "rules" for behavior. Of course, rules may well evolve from the conversation even if that was not the goal. When this happens, it would be best to frame the rules in nonreligious terms. For example, the Johnson & Johnson company is famous for its credo of ethical values that have underpinned corporate decisions since the company's inception. For many years, the credo included the phrase "with God's grace." But after a while management decided that some of J&J's employees might be uncomfortable with that terminology and removed it. For even though the values expressed in the credo were inspired by monotheistic ideas, the wording should be able to motivate any employee to live up to those values.

The Role of the Clergy

Clergymen and women can play a particularly important role in urging that religious ethics be brought to bear on economic decision making. But some significant changes in their training may be needed if they are to be more effective in that role than they have been to date.

Not long ago, a conference on business ethics was held at Princeton Theological Seminary. It was attended by high-ranking executives of Fortune 500–type corporations, accompanied by ministers, priests, and rabbis from their own churches and synagogues. At the end of the event, its sponsor observed: "One thing stood out boldly. The business leaders were largely innocent of biblical ethics as well as with the daily doings of congregation and denomination, and religious leaders were largely innocent of modern economics, as well as with the daily doings of a business."

I imagine that he would have said the same thing if the clergy in the audience had included Muslim imams or Buddhist monks. The problem begins, I think, in theological seminaries and other institutions of religious study. I have taken many classes with prospective ministers and rabbis. Most of them have been very bright and dedicated men and women. But with the exception of those who were coming into the ministry as a second career after spending time in business, most were rather innocent of the rough and tumble of global economic competition. Few had even studied economics as undergraduates, much less been exposed directly to the complex issues that businesspeople confront on a daily basis. Of course, people in many professions are lacking in business training, but few professionals have the unique responsibility that religious leaders have to offer moral guidance.

And what happens when these ministers-in-training leave the seminary? In many respects, they tend to lead a life that is more sheltered than the lives of those they minister to. As a result, they often are too quick to make moral generalizations that bear little relationship to the concrete circumstances that managers, salespeople, and others have to confront in the marketplace. I am reminded, here, of my minister friend who expressed concern that my focus on the "should nots" of religious ethics might not be proactive enough for God.

So there is a joint need. Not only do laypeople in the marketplace need a better understanding of religious ethics; clerics need a better understanding of marketplace realities. They need, somehow, to become engaged with the kinds of dialogues I have urged in the business world, and they need something else as well. They need to learn a lot more about religious traditions other than their own.

Ministers of all faiths will need to broaden their theological horizons if they want to be truly helpful in offering moral guidance to congregants. For those congregants are increasingly operating in a global marketplace. Consider, for example, a Christian minister whose congregant is about to be transferred to Saudi Arabia and asks for advice about the ethical challenges that he, and perhaps more importantly his wife, may confront in an Islamic society. It would not be terribly helpful for the minister to rely solely on a "What would Jesus do?" approach to the issues. The minister would be in a much better position to give helpful advice if he or she was knowledgeable about Islamic theology and traditions.

This can be a daunting, even terrifying, challenge for a clergyman or woman. To people of deep religious faith, delving into the tenets of other faiths can conjure up images of sacrificing their particular understandings of theological and moral truth on an altar of religious pluralism. I, personally, am a religious pluralist, believing that God's truth has multiple dimensions—that God speaks in many voices and in different times and places. But I can appreciate the fact that many of my friends in the clergy are not pluralists. Indeed, some say that my acceptance of pluralism is a sign of religious apathy, not religious conviction.

Yet the challenge cannot be avoided. If the clergy is to give helpful guidance to congregants who operate in a global marketplace, they must at least understand, even if they do not accept, how faiths other than their own have sought the truths of human existence. When they do, I believe that they will discover unexpected common ground. With that discovery, they will be able to give practical guidance for operating in a multicultural and multireligious business world without denying the particular truths that they hold dear. I hope that, in this book, I have shown how that may come about.

Works Cited and Other Sources

Scriptures and Foundational Documents Cited

Analects of Confucius. Translations and commentary:
D. C. Lau. London: Penguin Books, 1979.
Simon Ley. New York: W. W. Norton, 1997.
Bhagavad Gita. Translations and commentary:
Eliot Deutsch. New York: Holt Rinehart and Winston, 1968.
Barbara Stoller Miller. New York: Bantam Books, 1986.
Dhammapada. Translation and commentary:
Juan Mascaro. London: Penguin Books, 1973.
Hebrew Bible (Tanakh). Translation by Jewish Publication Society, 1989.
Hindu Scriptures (various). Translations and commentary:
Dominic Goodall. Berkeley: University of California Press, 1996.
Laws of Manu. Translation and commentary:
Wendy Doniger, and Brian K. Smith. London: Penguin Books, 1991.
Mishneh Torah of Maimonides. [Hebrew and English] New York: Feldheim, 1981.
New Testament. King James and New Revised Standard versions.
Papal Encyclicals and U.S. Bishops' Statements. In:
David J. O'Brien, and Thomas A. Shannon. *Catholic Social Thought: The Documentary Heritage.* Maryknoll, N.Y.: Orbis, 1992.
Qur'an. Translation:
Ahmed Ali. Princeton: Princeton University Press, 1994.
Ramayana. Translation and commentary:
Ranchor Prime. London: Collins & Brown, 1997.
Sermons of the Buddha. Translations and commentary:
Walpola Sri Rahula. *What the Buddha Taught*, 2nd edition. New York: Grove Press, 1974.

Buddhist Promoting Foundation. *The Teaching of Buddha.* Revised Edition. Tokyo: Kosaido, 1981.

Sermons and Essays of Reformation Leaders. In:

Max L. Stackhouse, et al., eds. *On Moral Business.* Grand Rapids: Eerdmans, 1995.

J. Philip Wogaman, and Douglas M. Strong, eds. *Readings in Christian Ethics: A Historical Sourcebook.* Louisville: Westminster/John Knox, 1996.

World Scriptures (*various*) with commentary. In:

Andrew Wilson, ed. *World Scripture: A Comparative Anthology of Sacred Texts.* St. Paul: Paragon, 1995.

Other Works Cited

Badaracco, Joseph L., Jr. *Defining Moments: When Managers Must Choose Between Right and Right.* Boston: Harvard Business School Press, 1997.

Boatright, John R. "Does Business Ethics Rest on a Mistake?" *Business Ethics Quarterly* (October 1999).

Carroll, Archie B. "Ethical Challenges for Business in the New Millennium." *Business Ethics Quarterly* (January 2000).

Carter, Stephen L. *The Culture of Disbelief: How American Law and Politics Trivializes Religious Devotion.* New York: Basic Books, 1993.

Chen, Li-Fiu. *The Confucian Way: A New and Systematic Study of "The Four Books."* Translated by Shun-Liu Shih. London: KPI/Routledge & Kegan Paul, 1986.

Chakraborty, S. K. *Ethics in Management: Vedantic Perspectives.* Delhi: Oxford University Press, 1995.

Chan, Wing Tsit, ed. *A Source Book in Chinese Philosophy.* Princeton: Princeton University Press, 1963.

Cox, Harvey. *The Secular City.* 25th Anniversary Edition. New York: Collier/ Macmillan, 1990.

Dalai Lama. *Ethics for the New Millennium.* New York: Riverhead, 1999.

Davis, Henry. *Moral and Pastoral Theology, Volume 2.* London: Sheed & Ward, 1935.

De Pree, Max. *Leadership Is an Art.* New York: Doubleday, 1989.

Eck, Diana L. *Encountering God: A Spiritual Journey from Bozeman to Banaras.* Boston: Beacon, 1993.

Friedman, Milton, and Rose Friedman. *Free to Choose: A Personal Statement*. New York: Harcourt Brace Jovanovich, 1980.

Gustafson, James M. *Protestant and Roman Catholic Ethics*. Chicago: University of Chicago Press, 1978.

Häring, Bernard. *The Law of Christ: Moral Theology for Priests and Laity*. Translated by Edwin G. Kaiser. Paramus, N.J.: Newman Press, 1966.

Hayek, F. A. *The Fatal Conceit: The Errors of Socialism*. Chicago: University of Chicago Press, 1989.

Herman, Stewart W., ed., with Arthur Gross Schaefer. *Spiritual Goods: Faith Traditions and the Practice of Business*. A Society for Business Ethics Anthology. Bowling Green, Oh.: Philosophy Documentation Center, 2001.

Herzog, Isaac. *The Main Institutions of Jewish Law*. Volume 2, *Law of Obligations*. 2nd edition. London: Soncino, 1967.

Heschel, Abraham J. *God in Search of Man*. New York: Harper & Row, 1956.

John Paul II. *Fides et Ratio: On The Relationship Between Faith and Reason*. Boston: Pauline Books & Media, 1998.

Keown, Damien. *Buddhism: A Very Short Introduction*. Oxford: Oxford University Press, 1996.

Kristol, Irving. *Two Cheers for Capitalism*. New York: Basic Books, 1978.

Mahoney, John. *The Making of Moral Theology: A Study of the Roman Catholic Tradition*. Oxford: Clarendon Press, 1987.

Meeks, M. Douglas. *God the Economist: The Doctrine of God and Political Economy*. Minneapolis: Fortress Press, 1989.

Mitroff, Ian I., and Elizabeth A. Denton. *A Spiritual Audit of Corporate America*. San Francisco: Jossey-Bass, 1999.

Morris, Tom. *If Aristotle Ran General Motors*. New York: Henry Holt, 1997.

Mottahedeh, Roy. *The Mantle of the Prophet: Religion and Politics in Iran*. New York: Pantheon, 1985.

Nash, Laura L. *Believers in Business*. Nashville: Thomas Nelson, 1994.

Nasr, Seyyed Hossein. *Traditional Islam in the Modern World*. London: KPI, 1987.

Queen, Christopher S., and Sallie B. King, eds. *Engaged Buddhism: Buddhist Liberation Movements in Asia*. Albany: State University of New York Press, 1996.

Qutb (Kotb), Sayed. *Social Justice in Islam*. New York: Octagon, 1970.

Sharma, Arvind, ed. *Our Religions*. San Francisco: Harper Collins, 1993.

Simon, Ernst. "The Neighbor (Re'a) Whom We Shall Love." In *Modern*

Jewish Ethics: Theory and Practice, edited by Marvin Fox. Columbus, Oh.: Ohio State University Press, 1975.

Stout, Jeffrey. *Ethics after Babel: The Languages of Morals and Their Discontents.* Boston: Beacon Press, 1988.

Tu, Wei-ming, ed. *Confucian Traditions in East Asian Modernity: Moral Education and Economic Culture in Japan and the Four Mini-Dragons.* Cambridge, Mass.: Harvard University Press, 1996.

Vickers, Geoffrey. *Value Systems and Social Process.* New York: Basic Books, 1968.

Walton, Clarence. *The Moral Manager.* New York: Harpers, 1988.

Walzer, Michael. *Spheres of Justice: A Defense of Pluralism and Equality.* New York: Basic Books, 1983.

Welch, D. Don. *Conflicting Agendas: Personal Morality in Institutional Settings.* Cleveland: Pilgrim Press, 1994.

Wilson, James Q. *The Moral Sense.* New York: Free Press, 1993.

Wilson, Rodney. *Economics, Ethics and Religion: Jewish, Christian and Muslim Economic Thought.* New York: New York University Press, 1997.

Wolfe, Alan. *Moral Freedom: The Search for Virtue in a World of Choice.* New York: W. W. Norton, 2001.

Selected Religious Sources Not Directly Cited

Jewish

Dorff, Elliot N., and Louis E. Newman, eds. *Contemporary Jewish Ethics and Morality: A Reader.* New York: Oxford University Press, 1995.

Elon, Menachem. *Jewish Law: History, Sources, Principles.* 4 volumes. Philadelphia: Jewish Publication Society, 1994.

Levine, Aaron. *Economic Public Policy and Jewish Law.* New York: Yeshiva University Press, 1993.

———. *Economics and Jewish Law: Halakhic Perspectives.* New York: Yeshiva University Press, 1987.

———. *Free Enterprise and Jewish Law.* New York: Yeshiva University Press, 1980.

Novak, David. *Jewish Social Ethics.* New York: Oxford University Press, 1992.

Pava, Moses L. *Business Ethics: A Jewish Perspective.* New York: Ktav/Yeshiva University Press, 1997.

Tamari, Meir. *With All Your Possessions: Jewish Ethics and Economic Life.* New York: Free Press, 1987.

Christian

Chappell, Tom. *The Soul of a Business: Managing for Profit and the Common Good.* New York: Bantam Books, 1993.

Childs, James M., Jr. *Ethics in Business: Faith at Work* Minneapolis: Fortress, 1995.

Grisez, Germain. *The Way of the Lord Jesus.* Volume 3, *Difficult Moral Questions.* Quincy, Ill.: Franciscan Press, 1997.

Herman, Stewart W. *Durable Goods: A Covenantal Ethics for Management and Employees.* Notre Dame, Ind.: University of Notre Dame Press, 1997.

Kuhn, James W., and Donald W. Shriver, Jr. *Beyond Success: Corporations and Their Critics in the 1900s.* New York: Oxford University Press, 1991.

Naylor, Thomas H., et al. *The Search for Meaning in the Workplace.* Nashville: Abingdon, 1996.

Nelson, Robert H. *Reaching for Heaven on Earth.* Lanham, Md.: Rowman & Littlefield, 1991.

Neuhaus, Richard John. *Doing Well and Doing Good: The Challenge to the Christian Capitalist.* New York: Doubleday, 1992.

Novak, Michael. *The Spirit of Democratic Capitalism.* 2nd edition. Lanham, Md.: Madison Books, 1991.

Stackhouse, Max L. *Public Theology and Political Economy: Christian Stewardship in Modern Society.* Lanham, Md.: University Press of America, 1991.

Troeltsch, Ernst. *The Social Teaching of the Christian Churches.* Reprint in two volumes. Louisville: Westminster/John Knox, 1992.

Weigel, George, and Robert Royal, eds. *A Century of Catholic Social Thought.* Washington, D.C.: Ethics and Public Policy Center, 1991.

Wogaman, J. Philip. *Christian Ethics: A Historical Introduction.* Louisville: Westminster/John Knox, 1993.

Islamic

Akhtar, Shabbir. *A Faith for All Seasons: Islam and the Challenge of the Modern World.* Chicago: Ivan R. Dee, 1990.

Denny, Frederick Mathewson. *An Introduction to Islam.* 2nd edition. New York: Macmillan, 1994.

Gambling, Trevor, and Rifaat Ahmed Abdul Karim. *Business and Accounting Ethics in Islam*. London: Mansell, 1991.

Khadduri, Majid. *al-Shafi'i's Risala*. Translation and Commentary. 2nd edition. Cambridge: Islamic Texts Society, 1987.

Rahman, Fazlur. *Major Themes of the Qur'an*. Minneapolis: Bibliotheca Islamica, 1980.

Saleh, Nabil A. *Unlawful Gain and Legitimate Profit in Islamic Law*. Cambridge: Cambridge University Press, 1986.

Serageldin, Ismail, "The Justly Balanced Society: One Muslim's View." In *Friday Morning Reflections at the World Bank*, edited by David Beckman et al. Washington, D.C.: Seven Locks Press, 1991.

Hindu, Buddhist, and Confucian

Coward, Harold, et al. "Responses to Problems of Population, Consumption, and Degradation of the Environment." *Journal of the American Academy of Religion* (summer 1997).

Fingarette, Herbert. *Confucius—The Secular as Sacred*. New York: Harper & Row, 1972.

Hall, David L., and Roger T. Ames. *Thinking through Confucius*. Albany: State University of New York Press, 1987.

Ivanhoe, Philip J. *Ethics in the Confucian Tradition: The Thought of Mencius and Wang Yang-ming*. Atlanta: Scholars Press, 1990.

Keown, Damien. *The Nature of Buddhist Ethics*. London: Macmillan, 1992.

Minor, Robert N., ed. *Modern Indian Interpretations of the Bhagavadgita*. Albany: State University of New York Press, 1986.

Reader, Ian. *Religion in Contemporary Japan*. Honolulu: University of Hawaii Press, 1991.

Rozman, Gilbert, ed. *The East Asian Region: Confucian Heritage and Its Modern Adaptation*. Princeton, N.J.: Princeton University Press, 1991.

Sizemore, Russell F., and Donald K. Swearer, eds. *Ethics, Wealth, and Salvation: A Study in Buddhist Social Ethics*. Columbia: South Carolina University Press, 1990.

Smith, Brian K. *Classifying the Universe: The Ancient Indian Varna System and the Origins of Caste*. New York: Oxford University Press, 1994.

Index